WINNERS
AND
LOSERS

Other Books by Jules Archer

African Firebrand: Kenyatta of Kenya
Angry Abolitionist: William Lloyd Garrison
Battlefield President: Dwight D. Eisenhower
China in the Twentieth Century
Chou En-lai
Colossus of Europe: Metternich
Congo
The Dictators
Epidemic!
The Executive "Success"
The Extremists: Gadflies of American Society
Famous Young Rebels
Fighting Journalist: Horace Greeley
From Whales to Dinosaurs
Front-Line General: Douglas MacArthur
Hawks, Doves, and the Eagle
Ho Chi Minh: The Legend of Hanoi
Hunger on Planet Earth
Indian Foe, Indian Friend
Laws That Changed America
Legacy of the Desert
Man of Steel: Joseph Stalin
Mao Tse-tung: A Biography
Mexico and the United States
1968: Year of Crisis
The Philippines' Fight for Freedom
The Plot to Seize the White House
Police State
Red Rebel: Tito of Yugoslavia
Resistance
Revolution in Our Time
Riot! A History of Mob Action in the United States
The Russians and the Americans
Strikes, Bombs, and Bullets: Big Bill Haywood and the I.W.W.
Superspies
Thorn in Our Flesh: Castro's Cuba
They Made a Revolution: 1776
Treason in America: Disloyalty Versus Dissent
Trotsky: World Revolutionary
Twentieth-Century Caesar: Benito Mussolini
Uneasy Friendship: France and the United States
The Unpopular Ones
Washington vs. Main Street
Watergate: America in Crisis
Who's Running Your Life?
World Citizen: Woodrow Wilson
You and the Law
You Can't Do That to Me!

WINNERS AND LOSERS

HOW ELECTIONS WORK IN AMERICA

JULES ARCHER

HARCOURT BRACE JOVANOVICH, PUBLISHERS
San Diego   New York   London

Fondly, for my delightful companions
Barbara Edell, Carolie Coffey,
Marilyn Steck, and Carla Wolfe

Requests for permission to make copies of any part of the work should
be mailed to: Permissions, Harcourt Brace Jovanovich, Publishers,
Orlando, Florida 32887

The author and publisher wish to thank the Library of Congress for
permission to reprint all photos that appear in this book, with the
exception of the photos on pages 6, 7, 16, 17, 21, 74, 89, 137, 154, and 174,
which appear courtesy of the Smithsonian Division of Political History; the
photo on page 64, which appears courtesy of the League of Women Voters;
and the photo on page 147, which appears courtesy of Washington State Archives.

Chapter 12 first appeared in somewhat different form
in *ADAM Magazine*, copyright © 1960 by Jules Archer.

Library of Congress Cataloging in Publication Data

Archer, Jules.
    Winners and losers: how elections work in America

Bibliography: p. 217-220
    Includes index.
    1. Elections—United States — Juvenile literature.
I. Title.
JK 1978.A72   1984   324.973   83-18368
ISBN 0-15-297945-X

Designed by Vaughn Andrews
Photo research by Patricia Stone Daniels
Photo captions by Susan Mihalic Tehrani
Printed in the United States of America

B   C   D   E

CONTENTS

✯═══✯═══ ACKNOWLEDGMENTS ✯═══✯═══

For their generous assistance in helping me to shed light on our intricate electoral system, to make it understandable and entertaining without being simplistic, I wish to thank:

My friend Professor Arthur Pearl of the University of California, himself once a candidate for Governor of Oregon; Jean G. Birch, Secretary, and William I. Greener III, Director of Communications, of the Republican National Committee; the National Teen Age Republicans (TARS); Rick Boylan of the Democratic National Committee; the Young Democrats of America; Raymond O. Heaps, G. W. Brown, and William K. Shearer of the American Independent Party; Donald Davis of the Socialist Workers Party; the Young Socialist Alliance; Robert Bills, National Secretary of the Socialist Labor Party; the AFL-CIO Committee on Political Education; and various individuals in Greece, Yugoslavia, France, Northern Ireland, England, and West Germany who discussed their countries' electoral systems with me.

My appreciation, too, to the Knight Publishing Corporation for allowing me to adapt my article "The Man Who Clowned His Way to the State Capitol" (*ADAM Magazine*), in somewhat different form, for Chapter 12 of this book.

Jules Archer
Santa Cruz, California

1

TEENAGE VOTING RIGHTS

Mouths fell open when fifteen-year-old Eric Salem of Lincoln, Nebraska, announced his intention to run for election as a board member of his county's Noxious Weed Control Authority. His reason: The mother of his best friend had been killed in an auto accident because her view of traffic at a corner had been obstructed by a large stand of weeds.

Two rivals for the post—one 37, the other 67—objected to letting a "kid" run against them. Finding nothing in the county's laws to stop him, they asked the state attorney general for a ruling. The answer came back: "It's legal—let him alone." The unusual spectacle of a fifteen-year-old running for public office against two adults fascinated the media.

News stories brought Eric $67 in campaign contributions, to which he added $300 of his own savings. Invited to speak to many local organizations, he also trudged from door to door, day after day, seeking people's support. On election day in Lincoln he received 20,000 votes, beating out both of his adult rivals to become probably the youngest person ever elected to public office in the United States.

Ironically, Eric couldn't even vote for himself. According to the Twenty-sixth Amendment to the Constitution, he had to wait three more years before he could cast a ballot in any general election. In fact, until 1971 you had to be at least 21. Congress then reduced the voting age to 18 because of protests by American youths being drafted for the

Vietnam War. TOO YOUNG TO VOTE FOR OUR LEADERS, read one demonstration banner, BUT NOT TOO YOUNG TO DIE FOR THEM.

The Twenty-sixth Amendment increased the size of the voting electorate by some 12 million young citizens. That was more than enough to play the decisive role in any election if the teenagers of America ever decided to vote as a solid bloc. Significantly, in the first year that eighteen-year-olds were able to vote, two American towns elected nineteen-year-old college students as mayors.

The potentially huge youth vote emphasizes the importance of citizenship training in junior high and high school. An impartial political course can equip you to vote intelligently, when you reach 18, in the best interests of your community, your nation, and yourself. This book represents a modest step in that direction.

Casting a vote is not the only way you can participate in elections. Even before you turn 18, you can help elect candidates you think deserve to be in office by joining their campaigns and working to win victory for them. Every political campaign has a welcome mat out for young volunteers.

Most of us believe that our precious right to vote was guaranteed by the Constitution and the Bill of Rights drafted by our Founding Fathers. Not so. Most of them were aristocrats who found it unthinkable to grant universal suffrage to the "common people." They considered the right to vote something to be granted only to "responsible" white males, especially those with property. Women were not to be taken seriously, of course, and as for blacks—savages!

Elitists like Alexander Hamilton had nightmares that universal suffrage would elect a rabble-rousing demagogue who would use the presidency to destroy the wealthy. The question of exactly who should be permitted to vote was left largely up to each state to determine as it chose.

States' rights were a sensitive issue. While the House of Representatives gave representation in Congress to people according to their numbers, the Senate was another story. The Founding Fathers were sensitive to the protests of smaller states that they would always be outvoted by states with bigger populations unless they had equality in the Senate. So each state was awarded only two senators, whether the state population was over 20 million, as in California today, or only 302,000, as in Alaska. Without this concession, the smaller original 13 colonies would never have agreed to give up their sovereignty to join the United States of America.

Our electoral system is remarkably elastic, able to accommodate the demands of drastically different interests. Candidates have to appeal to such diverse elements as Chicano farm workers, New York bankers, Denver police, Michigan farmers, Eskimo hunters, Texas oil rig workers, Pennsylvania coal miners, naturalized Cuban-American exiles in Miami, Mississippi River barge workers, San Francisco teachers, and Montana ranchers.

Voting patterns are changing as a result of the movement of millions of American families from cities and suburbs to small towns and rural areas, mainly in the South and West. When some localities tried to prevent newcomers from voting, the U.S. Supreme Court held in 1972 that one month was long enough to establish residency.

The swelling number of immigrants in the 1970's alarmed Congress into passing a new law requiring would-be voters to be able to read, write, and understand the English language. But when new elections liberalized Congress, the use of English literacy tests was suspended on grounds that immigrants could still understand the issues in elections through their own language newspapers.

Despite laws liberalizing voting rights, huge numbers of Americans don't bother going to the polls. In 1976 Jimmy Carter was elected President by only 27 percent of all Americans qualified to cast ballots. "Two thirds of our people do not even vote," he observed sadly. In 1977 the new governor of New Jersey was elected by only 15 percent of that state's qualified voters, while only 12 percent of qualified New Yorkers elected the mayor of their city. And in 1980 only 28 percent of qualified Americans elected Ronald Reagan President.

By contrast, up to 95 percent of qualified voters in Western Europe go to the polls to choose their representatives. Are Europeans more public-spirited? More aware of the benefits of voting one's choices?

Qualifications for voting are largely left to each state to determine,

3

provided they do not conflict with federal law. Thus in most states convicted felons are denied the vote even after they have paid for their offense. Many states have on their books dusty, obsolete laws curbing voting rights, which are not enforced. In California you can legally be barred from the polls for fighting a duel; in Florida for betting; in Vermont for disorderly conduct; in South Carolina for being a pauper; in Idaho for not owning property; and in Connecticut for not possessing a "good character."

In addition to voting in general elections, Americans 18 and over also have the right to vote in a *primary*—the contest within a political party to decide who will be its candidates in the general election. When you register to vote, most states require you to indicate which political party's next primary you wish to participate in. You can do so without being bound to vote for either the party or its candidates in the next general election. If you prefer, you can register with no party at all, abstaining from voting in any primary.

When you become a college student, a special voting problem may arise. Some towns in which colleges are located resent students voting there, influencing local issues, instead of voting in their home communities by absentee ballots. If you claim the college town as your true residence, you may be required to prove it by a local bank account, car registration, or tax return.

No youth 18 or older may be prevented from voting because of race or color (Fifteenth Amendment), sex (Nineteenth Amendment), or requirement to pay a poll tax of any kind (Twenty-fourth Amendment.)

From our earliest beginnings the right to vote did not come easily to all Americans. In the Massachusetts Bay Colony no colonist could vote unless he supported the Puritan Congregational Church and attended services regularly. Minister-teacher Roger Williams, banned from the colony as a dangerous radical, established the new colony of Rhode Island, where every man was granted the right to vote.

In the Virginia Colony of 1668, poor farmers were banned from the polls. They finally stormed the Virginia Assembly with muskets, forcing the terrified legislators to grant them suffrage on pain of death if the demand was rejected.

George Washington urged Congress to support public education throughout the country so that when the ballot was given to all men it would prove "a blessing and not a curse."

But John Adams was firmly opposed to extension of the voting privilege. "There will be no end of it . . ." he warned. "Women will demand a vote; lads from twelve to twenty-one will think their rights not enough attended to; and every man who has not a farthing will demand an equal voice. . . . It tends to . . . prostrate all ranks to one common level."

When he succeeded Washington as president, Adams moved swiftly to disenfranchise voters who supported his rival, Vice-President Thomas Jefferson. Aware that French- and Irish-Catholic refugees would vote for Jefferson's Democratic-Republican Party, Adams branded them "treasonous aliens." He ramrodded the Alien and Sedition Acts through Congress, making immigrants wait 14 years instead of five to become voting citizens.

The three groups of Americans who had to wait longest for the right to vote were ethnic minorities, teens, and women.

Before the Civil War, only five states in the whole country had allowed non-whites to vote. The Fifteenth Amendment, ratified in 1870, finally prohibited states from denying the vote to anyone "on account of race, color, or previous condition of servitude."

But discrimination persisted in many Southern states, which found other pretexts for barring blacks from the polls. They were refused ballots because they didn't have grandfathers who had voted; or hadn't paid a poll tax they couldn't afford; or couldn't pass a special literacy test forced on blacks alone; or hadn't voted in a primary election open only to whites. And there was always the threat of lynching by the Ku Klux Klan to deter any blacks brave enough to insist upon their voting rights.

In 1867 when federal troops were posted in Mississippi to enforce black suffrage, almost 67 percent of that state's blacks registered to vote. But when the troops were withdrawn in 1892, less than 6 percent of the blacks dared to register.

In 1904 Northern liberals in Congress sought to punish states that blocked blacks from voting by slashing their representation in Washington. But President Theodore Roosevelt crushed the move. If blacks were given an unqualified ballot, he declared, parts of the South

5

President Richard M. Nixon signs the 26th Amendment to the Constitution, lowering the voting age from 21 to 18. WHITE HOUSE PHOTO.

President John Adams feared that extending the voting privilege would "prostrate all ranks to one common level." LITHOGRAPH BY PENDLETON.

was denied the right to register to vote in California because of a discriminatory 1891 clause in the state constitution. It specified, "No person who shall not be able to read the Constitution in English . . . shall ever exercise the privileges of an elector in this State." Tens of thousands of Mexican-Americans in California had been barred from voting by that clause.

Ms. Castro happened to be literate in the Spanish language, and she could read a Spanish translation of the California constitution. She also had access to 18 Spanish-language newspapers and magazines, many of which carried discussions of political affairs. So she sued the state on behalf of all Spanish-speaking residents of Los Angeles County, claiming that the law barring them from voting violated their right to "equal protection under the law," as guaranteed by the Fourteenth Amendment.

The California Supreme Court awarded her the verdict, declaring, "It would indeed be ironic that petitioners . . . identified with the birth of California and contributing in no small measure to its growth, should be disenfranchised in their ancestral land, despite their capacity to cast an informed vote."

So today when you reach the age of 18 you have the right to vote whether you're male, female, poor, a newcomer, black, Indian, Hispanic, Asian, or any other kind of citizen.

2

YOUR RIGHT TO PARTICIPATE
AT ANY AGE—AND HOW

Even if you haven't reached voting age yet, you still have the right to participate in the election process in different ways and at different levels.

The early teens are a good time to begin getting involved in elections. I did myself when I was only 13, after becoming interested in the 1928 presidential race between Republican Herbert Hoover and Democrat Al Smith. At the time I felt strongly that Hoover would make the better president. So I began writing letters urging his support to the editor of the New York *World-Telegram*, then an important newspaper with over a million readers.

To my delight the editor—not realizing that I was only a thirteen-year-old boy—printed my long letters under bold headlines that dominated the editorial page. It was a thrill seeing my name in boldface type as the author; in fact, they gave me the incentive to continue with writing as a lifelong career. I have been an active political participant ever since.

I had no way of knowing how many of the paper's million-plus readers I influenced to vote for Hoover, but I received dozens of letters from people agreeing with me. That was how I, a mere slip of a youth without even a vote of my own, was able to make my voice heard in the 1928 elections.

That option still remains open today for young teens. In addition they will find the welcome mat out for them in youth groups sponsored by various political parties.

Teen Age Republicans (TARS) has some 120,000 teenage members in 50 state clubs. President Ronald Reagan credited them with having a significant impact on his election in 1980.

"You walked the precincts," he told them, "you licked stamps, stuffed envelopes, got senior citizens to the polls, and baby-sat while mothers voted. It may not sound very glamorous, but it's absolutely essential and especially in this era of campaign spending limitations. And often, what you did made the difference between winning and losing!"

TARS are trained for political leadership, over 85,000 having attended workshops dealing with current issues and with the specifics of campaign organization.

The Democrats sponsor a similar program, called Teen Dems, for young people in some 17 states. "The Teen Dem Clubs were utilized . . . to acquaint high school students with the principles of the Democratic Party and to interest them in politics," explained former Indiana Senator Birch Bayh. "They secured members of their own age group to help with . . . campaign chores. These young people, working after school hours, were extremely valuable to our Democratic organization, and I believe will become valuable workers for the senior party in later years."

Teens who get high on politics can wield an amazing amount of clout. When Oregon prepared to hold presidential primary elections in 1964, Sunset High School students in Beaverton decided to stage a mock Republican primary. They invited Governor Nelson Rockefeller of New York, then a presidential candidate, to be their keynote speaker. To their delight he accepted and showed up in Beaverton (pop. 5,937). The Oregon press played up the story, and when Rockefeller won the state primary he credited his victory to the students of Sunset High.

Getting involved in politics as a teenager, you could find yourself occupying a more important position in an election campaign than you ever imagined possible. When Illinois Senator Charles Percy first ran for office, he chose as manager of one of his Chicago campaign centers a bright eighteen-year-old boy who did a superb job for the candidate, who emerged victorious.

Edward Bouchet was only 25 when he ran for the Rhode Island Senate. People laughed when he made his seventeen-year-old sister his campaign manager. But she mustered an enthusiastic corps of supporters from her high school. With the aid of 75 of them, she steered her brother to victory.

Over 200 high school political clubs supported the campaign of Senator Howard Baker of Tennessee. "The enthusiastic participation in our campaign by the young people of our state," he declared, "was the single most important factor in our success."

Former Senator George McGovern of South Dakota also credited high school students for his senatorial victories "by doing precinct organizational work, mass mailing preparation, maintaining the campaign headquarters, and the thousand and one other tasks that inevitably come up in any bid for political office."

The AFL-CIO Committee on Political Education (COPE) welcomes teenage volunteers interested in electing pro-labor candidates. They seek youngsters who can spare anything from an hour to a few days a week to telephone, canvass door-to-door, type precinct lists, keep card files up-to-date, check registrations, canvass voters on their choices, distribute handbills, post election notices, and help get voters to the polls.

Even if you don't join a political campaign, you can still get involved in the electoral process that most directly affects you—in your own school. Most schools have student councils. By winning election to one of these, a student gets a voice in the rules and conditions governing the school day.

"Students in school as well as out," the U.S. Supreme Court has ruled, "are 'persons' under our Constitution . . . [and] possessed of fundamental rights which the state must respect."

According to the American Civil Liberties Union, students and student organizations must be allowed to hold meetings in schoolrooms and auditoriums, or on school grounds, to discuss freely, and pass resolutions about, any matter concerning them. In court cases students have won the right to distribute political campaign literature at high schools and to collect signatures on petitions.

One group of New York high school students formed a City General Organization Council, claiming to represent some 275,000 students who demanded a voice in educational policies. They called for representative student government in each school "free from domination by the administration and faculty adviser." When the Council's president, seventeen-year-old Donald St. George Reeves, protested cuts in the school budget, he was suspended. But he was reinstated the next day when several hundred students demonstrated in his support.

Responding to the youthful Council's pressure, the New York Board of Education issued directives ordering every high school to organize "an elective and truly representative student government," with all students allowed to form political organizations and vote. This government was also given the power to allocate student activity funds and participate in making decisions "in certain areas, including curriculum and disciplinary policies." Many school boards have since followed suit.

Political-science teacher Steven Teel of Berkeley High School, California, sought to give his students a better understanding of our political system. He turned his classes into a mock Senate and House of Representatives for a whole term, with each student impersonating a real senator or congressman. Learning how to process bills into law, many students developed a deep interest in politics. Some began to think of running as real candidates in future elections.

You might even consider running for a seat on your local school board. In New York, Susan Spencer, an eighteen-year-old senior at Linton High School, ran for election to a vacancy on the school board. Her name was banned from the voting machines, however, when State Attorney General Louis J. Lefkowitz issued an opinion that no one under 21 could hold elective office.

Susan fought the action in court. The State Supreme Court ruled that the election had been illegal because Susan had been excluded, and ordered the local board of education to hold a new election in which she could run. Subsequently the New York legislature passed a new law permitting persons under 21 to run for elective public office.

Students who get involved in school politics and elections are likely to enjoy participating in local, state, and national elections as well. Their experience with the details of campaigning makes them especially welcome in the headquarters of political candidates.

There are special rewards for getting involved in political campaigns. You have the satisfaction of accomplishing an important goal. You enjoy the pleasure of working together with others who feel as you do about the candidate and the issues. You earn respect from them by your participation. You're often invited to hear and meet leading political figures. And you acquire a behind-the-scenes understanding of what goes on in American politics and how elections work.

Teenagers are often more welcome than adults in campaign headquarters because adults are more likely to be bored with routine jobs like phoning prospective voters or addressing envelopes, while teens tend to be cheerfully eager to do whatever is necessary to help their candidate win the election. Working together, they make even the dullest of chores fun.

"The importance of young volunteers cannot be overemphasized," observed former Senator Philip Hart of Michigan. "No one else has their enthusiasm and their tireless energy and their willingness to do anything and everything. No campaign could function without such a devoted band. But on the other hand the volunteers get as much from campaigning as they give, and I hope and believe they find it a rewarding experience."

Participating in a campaign also gives you the chance to meet people who can be helpful in developing a political career of your own. If an influential person becomes impressed with you, he or she can open doors for you that can launch you on your way.

A Texas youngster who arrived in Washington as a Congressional aide came to the attention of President Franklin D. Roosevelt. The President selected him to be an official in the National Youth Administration. That was the beginning of a skyrocketing political career that took Lyndon B. Johnson all the way to the White House.

As in any other field of endeavor, when you get your foot inside the door in any capacity, anything can happen.

Mark Hatfield was only ten years old when he passed out handbills asking voters to reelect Hoover in 1932. That was the beginning of a political career that first made Hatfield governor of Oregon, then a United States senator.

"I have been fortunate in having many young people volunteer in my campaigns," declared former Utah Senator Frank Moss, "and my debt to them is great. I have found also that some of the boys and girls who worked for me in past campaigns, and who continued working in politics when they were able to vote, are now candidates in their own right."

Political candidates are often surprisingly successful at very young ages. Early on, Roger Bedford of Alabama participated enthusiastically in many political campaigns. Then, at age 26 he decided to run for the state senate. Winning an upset victory, he became the youngest senator ever to sit in that statehouse.

When law student Paul Soglin was arrested in the late sixties for taking part in a peace demonstration in Madison, Wisconsin, the police force of conservative Mayor William Dyke forcibly shaved off his long hair. Paul never forgot that humiliation. Four years later he organized a coalition of students, anti-war activists, minorities, and labor groups. Running against Dyke for mayor, he won and dumped that chagrined official out of office.

Participating in an election campaign can also open other career doors for you. Suppose, for example, that you aspire to write the speeches that candidates deliver on the campaign trail. If you volunteer to do office work for a candidate, you'll get a chance to meet his or her speech writers. They'll appreciate your offer to do research for them in the library and help them bang out some speeches. If you do a good job, you might end up as a paid writer of campaign speeches.

Working for the election of a successful candidate, you could also possibly win a summer internship in Washington, working in a congressional office or government agency. Thousands of such jobs with pay are available each summer, invaluable training for anyone interested in a political career.

Girls today have greater opportunities in the political arena than ever before, and they need not hesitate to get involved.

Before Harriet Keyserling of South Carolina ran for her first office in county government, she was active as an observer for the League of

President Lyndon B. Johnson
began his national political
career as a youthful Congressional
aide.

Young people can influence the
outcome of elections through
distributing party literature.

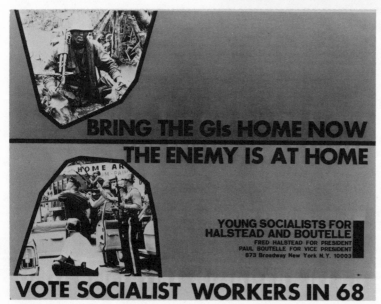

These five young people ran for the Ann Arbor, Michigan City Council in 1972, as members of the Human Rights Party.

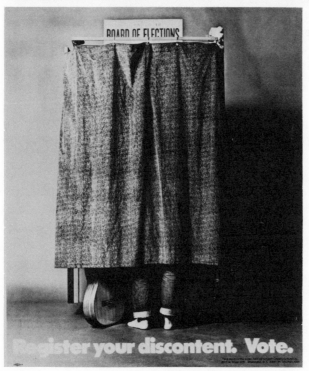

The type of government you have is your decision.

Women Voters. "While observing County Council one day," she recalled, "I thought, 'I can do that as well as, or better than, some of them.'" Running for a seat on the council, she won. Then she went on to win election to the South Carolina House of Representatives.

Keyserling advises women not to be too self-critical. "Just look around you," she suggests. "Can't you really do as well as, or even better than, at least half the people now in office?"

A 1977 survey showed that nationally some 19 percent of city council members were women, and in California 23 percent of school trustees were women.

During California elections in 1976, 31 women ran for office on major party tickets. Eight were elected to seats in Congress, the State Senate, and the State Assembly.

Representation of the sexes in the nation's governing bodies is still far from equal. Nevertheless more and more women are winning public office in every election.

Women can also participate in politics by joining such organizations as the National Women's Political Caucus, the League of Women Voters, the National Organization for Women, the Women's Campaign Fund (which provides money and help to female candidates), and special groups campaigning for or against the Equal Rights Amendment (ERA), abortion on demand, and prayer in the public schools.

In the final analysis, what kind of government you have is up to you. If you want change, you won't get it by just complaining to your friends. As an individual you may feel powerless to influence your government. But *collectively* you can have tremendous impact. And the way to begin is to get a small ground swell started in the neighborhood, district, or town where you live.

3

WHY ELECTIONS ARE
IMPORTANT TO YOU
—NOW AND TOMORROW

"*I* am the law!" boasted Jersey City Mayor Frank Hague, political boss of New Jersey during the 1930's. He controlled the state's corrupt political machine, which rigged elections. His goon squads beat up, jailed, or ran out of town anyone who dared oppose or challenge his iron rule. Excitement ran high when two congressmen declared they were coming to Jersey City to defy his ban on free speech.

As a young New Yorker then, I crossed the Hudson River with a friend to attend their rally. What we saw in Journal Square frightened us. Hague's burly goons had set up roadblocks to keep the congressmen out. They roamed the square snooping into out-of-town cars, eavesdropping on groups waiting to hear the congressmen, and abruptly seizing and running out of town any "undesirables." Police were invisible.

The atmosphere was tense and fraught with violence.

"I've been in Nazi Germany," one man near us suddenly shouted in angry defiance, "and this is ten times worse!" Hague's henchmen promptly pounced on him and dragged him out of sight.

After that my friend and I spoke only in careful whispers.

Word finally spread that the two congressmen had been persuaded to call off their trip because of the danger to their lives. My friend and I left Jersey City quickly. When we reached the New York side of the border, we whooped and hollered in tremendous relief, shouting, "Hooray for New York! Hooray for democracy!"

That was a taste of what can happen even in the United States—and from time to time has happened—when voters lose control of their state to a corrupt, dangerous political boss. As a result of my chilling experience in Hague's New Jersey, I joined the American League Against War and Fascism to work politically against other attempts to sabotage the democratic processes that protect our liberties.

Similarly, it was no coincidence that youth was in the forefront of the widespread protest movements of the 1960's and 1970's. Young people are always the most idealistic and energetic generation, because it is mostly their future that is at stake.

Most of us older Americans tend to blame the government when things go wrong in the country, without reflecting that our own votes—or more often, the lack of them—put incompetents in power. Unfortunately many of us are too busy with our jobs, our families, and our recreation to pay much attention to the news or to analyze the political issues of the day.

As a result, out of Americans eligible to vote, only 25 to 30 percent exercise their right of suffrage with any degree of regularity. Another 30 to 40 percent vote so infrequently as to have negligible influence on the electoral process. Thus only a tiny minority of Americans select the candidates who run for and win over 500,000 elective offices in the United States.

The ancient Greeks, who invented democracy as a political system, held that political authority must remain in the hands of the people, not in any ruler's. Since there are too many of us to rule ourselves directly, we elect representatives to enact or revoke our laws. But when those representatives are elected by only a third of Americans, do we really have a democracy?

In contrast, a country like Australia insists that voting is a civic duty, not just a privilege. Anyone who, without a good reason, fails to vote is subject to a fine. Australia, consequently, has one of the highest voting turnouts in the world. This guarantees that their elected officials really represent the will of the vast majority. Critics of compulsory voting, however, doubt that it is any guarantee of better government because it drives to the polls many voters who don't really understand the issues.

The question of who "really" understands the issues in an election campaign is a value judgment. Democrats are convinced that Republi-

Frank Hague, the corrupt, dangerous political boss of New Jersey in the 1930's.

A 1972 poster, picturing a young man who participated in the 1965 Selma, Alabama Voting Rights March. Young people, it is predicted, will soon become a majority of the voting population.

cans blindly vote for issues that will turn the clock back to 1920. Republicans are convinced that Democrats don't realize their programs will bankrupt the country.

Our system nevertheless urges both to vote their choices. The larger the vote, the more clearly the will of the citizens is manifested.

Election issues can be of supreme importance to every American. The candidates we elect to Congress and the White House can keep us at peace or embroil us in a war overseas, with all the anguish and terror war brings. William Lloyd Garrison, the famous abolitionist, mocked his fellow countrymen for singing the praises of peace while electing military presidents.

Even when voters are not well informed, the ballot in their hands is less dangerous to our society than any attempt to deprive them of it by some kind of qualification test. Whenever citizens are denied the right to vote for who governs them and how, you have a dictatorship, not a democracy. If people are not given the opportunity to get rid of officials by voting them out of office, they may become desperate enough to do it the only other way possible—by violent revolution.

America's young people, who are expected soon to become a majority of the voting population, need to become aware of the crucial issues of our society if they are to vote intelligently.

"The schools, in their fundamental obligation to prepare youth for citizenship, have failed completely," thinks Professor of Education Arthur Pearl, University of California, Santa Cruz. "Schools continue to be places . . . where children go to learn how to become stupid about war, economics, labor, minorities, poverty, and communism. . . . Thus it is possible for a candidate to prate about economies leading to savings of *millions* of dollars in cutbacks in welfare benefits, school children's lunches, or excesses in poverty programs, while almost in the same breath he may ask for *billions* of dollars more . . . for military expenditures."

If America is to have a bright future, young people need to understand the whole truth about our past as a nation. When they do, they will know how to recognize and avoid mistakes made in the past, while voting to uphold and advance the best traditions in our history.

Too often, however, our schools have given us a simplistic, dressed-up version of our history in the belief that patriotism requires young people to think of our country as always being in the right. But *all* nations make mistakes, and we are no exception. Unless we learn from our mistakes, we are likely to repeat them.

In 1972 an estimated 25 million new young voters became entitled to the ballot for the first time. The National Association of Student Governments announced the formation of a "National Youth Caucus" to get student activists into power on the local level of every state, where they could influence that year's presidential elections.

This was supposed to be a problem for the Nixon administration, which most high school and college students opposed because of its persistence in prosecuting the Vietnam War. But the Nixon administration did not take the notion of a united "youth vote" very seriously.

"The thinking here is that the young people who vote for the first time in '72 will split more or less along the same old lines as their parents," observed campaign correspondent Hunter S. Thompson. "'How many will even register?' they ask. 'And even then—even assuming a third of the *possibles* might register, how many of those will actually get out and vote?' The implication, every time, is that the 'youth vote' is just a noisy paper tiger."

Nixon's reelection seemed to validate that prophecy.

The Vietnam War and the Watergate scandal contributed to making many older Americans, as well, cynical about politics. In a book called *A Tide of Discontent*, Clifton McClesky observed that from 1964 to 1978 the number of people who trusted the government to do what was right plummeted from 76 to 29 percent. The number who felt that a few big-business interests controlled the government rose from 24 to 65 percent.

The growing disinterest of Americans in elections was dramatized sharply in 1980 when, in an election year, President Jimmy Carter bought half an hour of TV time to tell why he felt he ought to be re-elected. Only one American in 25 was willing to listen. Two weeks later when his chief rival for the Democratic nomination, Senator Edward Kennedy, took half an hour on TV to discuss vital problems confronting the nation, he talked to just 10 million Americans. Hours later when the Super Bowl football game was broadcast, 105 million tuned in.

Americans who don't bother voting often excuse their apathy by saying, "It doesn't matter who gets elected, because all politicians are just a bunch of crooks."

"When a man says to me that politics is dirty," Woodrow Wilson told a New Jersey audience in 1912, "I ask him if he voted at the last primary. If he says that he didn't, I invite him to shut up!"

Politics is neither automatically clean nor dirty. It is exactly what we, the voters, make it—just as businesses, churches, labor unions, and other American institutions are what their constituents make them. If most of us refuse to get involved in politics, we leave it to a few unscrupulous people eager to control it for their own selfish ends.

Who, then, is really to blame?

The candidates who win election to public office have the power to change your life by the laws they pass. Does it make sense to entrust so much power to persons you don't know anything about? Whom you've had no say in electing?

Political activist Dick Gregory is convinced that youth offers the best hope for solving our national problems. "We can expect to see some real change in the political life of the United States," he believes. "The number-one thing young people in America—indeed, young people around the world—have going for them is their sense of honesty, morality, and ethics. Young people refuse to accept the lies and rationalizations of the established order. They will be looking for candidates who are honest, candidates who have a moral vision, candidates who are concerned more with solving social problems than they are with merely winning an election."

How can you select such candidates to vote or work for?

First, listen to what all the candidates have to say and read the literature distributed by their headquarters. Read about them in newspapers and magazines. Discuss them with friends, family, and other people whose opinions you respect. Check the recommendations of impartial political organizations, such as the League of Women Voters.

When you've made up your mind, it makes sense to get involved in the campaigns of the candidates whose views you support, even if you're not yet of voting age. Laws affecting your future life will be made either by them or by candidates whose ideas may be opposed to yours.

Those laws can decide whether you will be faced with the threat of nuclear war; whether you can be drafted to fight a foreign war; how much tax you will have to pay out of your salary; whether you will have a job and what kind; how much you will have to pay for imported cars and motorcycles or for food; whether you will be able to afford your own home; whether your savings will be safe in the banks; whether the school system will improve or get worse; whether you can get financial help to go to college; whether prayer will be introduced in your local schools; whether you will be forced to live with polluted air and water; whether there will be a new energy shortage.

These problems won't go away quickly, and they won't solve themselves. You may have to deal with them for the rest of your life. You have every reason, therefore, to get involved in electing the kind of candidates who convince you they have intelligent plans and the ability to help solve those problems.

By participating in the political life of your community, you also forge common bonds of interest with others who have the same concerns. That is your best weapon against feeling powerless in local issues directly affecting you.

In 1970 the town leaders of Trenton, Maine, were ready to license the building of a nuclear power plant and an aluminum factory to bring jobs to the town. Despite the need for those jobs and the tax relief the new industries would provide, the little town's citizens were vehemently opposed to allowing the pollution they knew would poison their environment. Banding together against the town officials, they forced the issue to be put on a ballot, and they defeated it by a vote of 144 to 77.

There's a lot at stake for you in elections—local, state, and national. The earlier in your life that you get involved, the better the chance that you and your generation can create an American future closer to your heart's desire.

And when you have the vote, remember the late Martin Luther King's advice, born of a lifetime of struggle:

"The most important step that a person can take is that short walk to the ballot box."

4

HOW THE SYSTEM WORKS

When Ronald Reagan and George Bush challenged each other for the Republican presidential nomination in 1980, Reagan proclaimed his plans for improving economic conditions. Bush sneered at his program as nonsense—"voodoo economics."

Politics makes strange bedfellows. When Reagan won the nomination, he chose as his running mate none other than his detractor, George Bush. Bush, in turn, had no qualms about accepting the vice-presidential nomination that pledged him to endorse the very "voodoo economics" he had derided.

"So what?" laughed one Republican delegate. "Nobody takes seriously what one candidate says about another when they're both fighting for the nomination."

President Jimmy Carter, the Democratic opposition candidate, was quick to quote Bush's view of Reagan's "voodoo economics" during the ensuing campaign. Voters nevertheless elected the Republican ticket.

One of the odd ways in which our system works is that a party's rival candidates for an office will often attack each other as harshly as if they were members of different parties. Afterward, however, party loyalty requires them to reconcile, with the loser campaigning for the winner against the candidate of the opposition party.

As established by Congress in 1845, we elect our presidents on the

Tuesday after the first Monday in November. On this day Americans also vote for many members of Congress and for state and municipal candidates as well.

Elections held halfway in a president's four-year term are called off-year or mid-term elections. In these we vote for all 435 representatives, about a third of the senators, about half the state governors, and many state and local officeholders. Mid-term elections are often viewed as a vote of confidence in, or repudiation of, the president's policies, depending on how well his party does at the polls.

The national candidates for whom you can vote to serve you in Washington are the president, vice-president, two senators, and a congressman. The state candidates for whom you can vote include a governor, lieutenant governor, other state officials, and members of your state legislature. The town and county candidates you vote for may include a mayor, sheriff, city councilpersons, and school-board members.

Each state has the right to decide how to hold its elections, as long as this does not conflict with federal requirements. Thus one state may hold elections for governor every four years, while another will elect a new governor every two years. Each state is entitled to elect two U.S. senators for six-year terms and members of the House of Representatives every two years, in numbers proportionate to the population.

The Founding Fathers arranged this plan to create a balance between the popular will and states' rights. If all our laws were passed simply by popular vote, the people of New York, with 34 representatives, would have 34 times as much power in Congress as the people of South Dakota, who have only one. But in the Senate, South Dakota has equal power with New York, each state having two senators apiece.

Many people are confused about the difference between primary and general elections. "A good many political-science professors and government teachers never taught people the difference . . ." observed Louise Lindblom, 1982 Executive Director, Alabama State Democratic Committee. "People do not understand that a primary is a party matter for the purpose of nominating a candidate for the general election ballot in November."

The voting process begins with your registration at a designated place. Election officials and poll watchers are entitled to check your name and address to make sure you are qualified in terms of age, citizenship, and length and place of residence, as well as to make certain you vote only once.

You may register as a Democrat, Republican, Socialist, or member of any other party, or as an independent. No matter how you register, you can vote any way you please in the general election. But if you register as a member of a particular party, you are then entitled to vote in its state primary to select its next candidates for the general election.

A few states hold open primaries in which you can vote without prior registration, provided you don't vote in the primary of more than one party.

State primary results are watched carefully by national party leaders because they indicate the popularity of various party candidates. Thus if John Smarthead emerges as the favorite presidential choice in the first five or six state primaries, he may become the party's "front-runner" candidate, likely to win substantial support at the party's national convention, which will choose the final candidate.

State primaries also test whether or not a candidate has liabilities that may hurt him in a national election. When John F. Kennedy sought the presidency in 1960, many Democratic leaders opposed his nomination because they felt that Americans would never elect a Roman Catholic to the White House. But they were forced to sit up and take notice when he entered the early West Virginia Democratic primary and emerged the victor in that almost entirely Protestant state.

Still there were reservations about Kennedy's youth. He entered six more state primaries and won them all, making himself the front-runner who deserved—and won—the nomination at the Democratic Party's national convention.

A candidate can win primary after primary and still be denied his party's presidential nomination at the national convention. In 1952 Senator Estes Kefauver emerged from the primaries as the most popular Democratic candidate. Yet the convention nominated instead Adlai Stevenson, who had entered no primaries at all. This happened again in 1968 when Vice-President Hubert Humphrey, who had avoided all primaries, was chosen over Senator Eugene McCarthy, a winner in the primaries.

A candidate's showing in the primaries is only one factor influencing the choice of convention delegates. A public-opinion poll showing that a candidate is likely to beat the other party's front-runner can help him or her enormously. Some candidates also spend several years before the national convention doing favors for party leaders in many states, counting on their support in return when they lead delegations to the convention.

Little more than one in three states holds a primary. "I hope that people have had a bellyful of these primaries," said former President Harry S Truman in 1960. "They are outrageously expensive and exhausting." States without primaries use any method they wish to select delegates to the national convention.

Until the 1970's most delegates were chosen at closed party gatherings called *precinct caucuses*. About a third are still chosen in this manner. A 1967 survey by the League of Women Voters revealed that in many states only a handful of party loyalists showed up at the caucuses. When one Arizona party invited 500 members to attend, only a dozen appeared. That two percent of the party's membership then selected national delegates on behalf of the whole party in Arizona.

When all parties select their nominees at their conventions, state candidates as well as national, you may be dissatisfied with all their choices. You always have the option to write in on your ballot the name of any unlisted candidate you prefer. It is rare that a candidate is elected by this method, but it serves as a protest vote. Poll officials are required to show you how to cast a write-in vote, upon your request.

The smallest voting units in a state are called *precincts* or *districts*. In most states these are grouped into *wards*. But the voting structure differs from state to state. The best way to understand how it works in your state is to join a local political club and take part in an election campaign.

Ward or precinct captains were once powerful figures in our electoral system. Before the introduction of our present-day welfare system, America's poor felt compelled to turn for assistance to city or county political organizations. The ward or precinct captains responded by providing coal, warm clothing, baskets of groceries, and persuasion for landlords to hold off on the rent.

Recipients of this largesse expressed their gratitude by voting into office the choices of the ward politicians, who were frequently repaid by opportunities to plunder city and state treasuries through graft. Loyal party workers were rewarded with government jobs and could be counted on to lead family and friends to the polls to keep the party in power.

In old turn-of-the-century New York, the corrupt Tammany Hall political machine was famous for its skill in mustering votes. A ward boss named Plunkett explained, "I know every man, woman, and child in the Fifteenth District. . . . I know what they like and what they don't like. . . . I hear of a young feller that's proud of his voice . . . I ask him to come around to Washington Hall and join our glee club. . . . Another young feller gains a reputation as a baseball player in a vacant lot. I bring him into our baseball club. . . . I rope them all in by givin' them opportunities to show themselves off. I don't trouble with political arguments. I just study human nature and act accordin'."

As in Plunkett's day, some voters still vote as they do because of favors received or expected from a candidate's political apparatus. But most Americans today cast their ballots for candidates who most closely approximate their own views and whose election they feel will benefit them personally as well as being good for the country.

There is a great deal of bloc voting for candidates because they are of the same race, religion, or ethnic origin. The 1980 census found that one in five Americans belong to some minority group—26.5 million blacks, 14.6 million Hispanics, 3.5 million Asians, 1.4 million native Americans and Eskimoes.

Black Americans tend to vote as a bloc either for black candidates or for white candidates pledged to remedy black grievances. They usually vote the Democratic ticket in the conviction that this party is more sympathetic to black problems and has done more about them. At the same time, many blacks feel that they are not getting their fair share of elective offices. Constituting about 11 percent of the population, they represent only one percent of elected officials. Pointing out that a solid black vote can tip any election, black leaders have warned both the Democratic and Republican Parties that they must either nominate more black candidates or have black candidates run independently against them.

Not so long ago black leaders who merely tried to get blacks to the voting booths did so at the peril of their lives. In June, 1963, Douglas MacArthur Cotton and eight other members of the Student Nonviolent Coordinating Committee (SNCC) attempted to lead 200 black citizens of Greenwood, Mississippi, to the courthouse to register them to vote. Arrested for "disturbing the peace," they were given a five-minute trial without permission to obtain an attorney and were sentenced to $200 fines and four months' hard labor at a county farm.

Mistreated by guards, they went on a work and hunger strike in protest. They were punished by transfer to Parchman State Penitentiary, where they were put in a "hot box"—a windowless, lightless closet—and kept locked there for two scorching days and nights. Several collapsed. Later Cotton was hung by his hands from the cell bars for three hours.

The black students were finally bailed out after 55 days, and Cotton was threatened with being shot if he returned.

All this punishment was for asserting the right to vote for 200 black citizens of Greenwood, Mississippi. The civil rights acts of the Johnson administration ended such blatant miscarriages of justice.

In addition to the black vote, politicians are also sensitive to other voting blocs that play an important election role in certain states. Among these are the strong "Jewish vote" in California, Florida, and New York; the "Irish and Greek vote" in Massachusetts; the "Portuguese vote" in Rhode Island; the "Cajun vote" in Louisiana; and the "French-Canadian vote" in Maine and New Hampshire.

Jewish-American voters have their own special interests. For many these include the state of Israel; candidates sympathetic to the Palestinian cause instead may find a heavy Jewish vote cast against them. Jewish constituents also tend to vote solidly for Jewish candidates, so that in 1980 no fewer than 8 out of 100 U.S. Senators were of Jewish heritage. Like the blacks, most Jewish voters vote Democratic, considering it the more liberal of the two major parties. Nevertheless they voted as enthusiastically for Republican Dwight Eisenhower as they did for Democrat John F. Kennedy.

Other minority groups also tend to vote for candidates of their own ethnic origin. In 1982, for example, Italian-American voters elected almost 30 Italian-American representatives to Congress. Hispanic

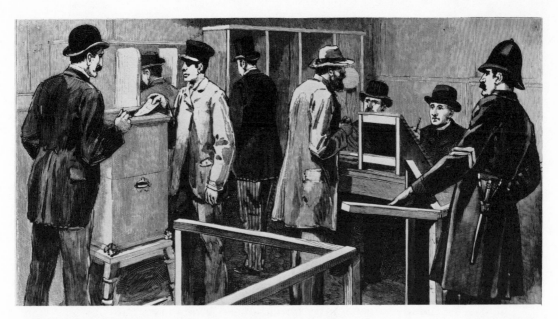

A drawing depicting the voting process in 1889.
WOOD ENGRAVING FROM *FRANK LESLIE'S ILLUSTRATED NEWSPAPER.*

Two North Dakota farmers read the ballots posted outside a schoolhouse on election day in 1940. Politicians must be sensitive to the needs of many voting blocs. PHOTO BY JOHN VACHON.

Adam Clayton Powell and the New York delegation in 1942, on their way to protest the poll tax filibuster. Poll taxes were one method employed to keep blacks from voting. PHOTO BY GORDON PARKS.

voters in California made their weight felt by compelling the state's public schools to adopt a policy of bilingual education.

When you vote for national, state, or local candidates in a general election, your vote counts directly—except for two political offices, those of president and vice-president. Although millions of Americans think they are voting directly for candidates for those two offices, in fact they are voting for members of an Electoral College who cast the official vote. This "college" has no building or campus. The victorious electors of each state simply meet in their state capitol.

They represent only the party receiving the highest presidential vote in that state. They are usually first chosen at their party's state convention from among influential and prominent party members. Each state is guaranteed the same number of electors as it has members in Congress. No state has less than three, but states with the largest populations have the largest number of votes in the Electoral College.

The electors meet on the first Monday after the second Wednesday in December. By long-established custom they vote for their party's nominees, usually the candidates who have won a majority of the popular vote, although the electors are not specifically required to do so by law.

All of a state's electoral votes are awarded to the winners of that state's election race. Then all the states' results are tallied. The presidential team receiving a majority of the Electoral College votes is officially proclaimed the winner of the election. If no team has a clear majority, however, because of third-party votes, the election is then thrown into the House of Representatives. They select a president from among the three candidates with the highest Electoral College vote. In that case, all the congressmen of each state must combine their votes to cast a single ballot.

If the Electoral College fails to give a majority to any of the vice-presidential nominees, then the Senate chooses from the two with the highest votes, each senator casting a single vote.

A presidential candidate can actually receive a majority of the votes cast in the nation and still lose the election if the Electoral College votes for someone else. Three presidents have gone to the White House with fewer votes than their opponents. In 1824 Andrew Jackson received over 43 percent of the popular vote, and John Quincy Adams less than 31 percent, but the Electoral College still elected Adams.

In 1876 Samuel J. Tilden won almost 51 percent of the popular vote, compared to Rutherford B. Hayes' 48 percent, yet by one vote the Electoral College made Hayes president. And in 1888 Grover Cleveland won more of the popular vote than Benjamin Harrison, but the Electoral College put Harrison in the White House instead.

These were isolated instances, however, and today it is taken for granted that the presidential team that wins the largest vote in the popular election will automatically win the Electoral College vote. The presumption is that the College is morally obligated to follow the will of the people. But the election is not official until the Electoral College announces its choices.

It should be noted, too, that a presidential candidate can be elected without winning a majority of the popular vote. This happened to 15 of our presidents. All they needed was the *highest* vote given to any of three or more candidates, even if it was less than 50 percent. Consequently they became presidents with the majority of American voters having voted against them.

With all these flaws, the remarkable thing about our electoral system is that it works as well as it does.

5

HOW WE GOT THAT WAY

The first presidential convention and the first campaign hoopla took place in 1828 during the election race between Andrew Jackson and John Quincy Adams. Jackson, a former frontiersman born in a log cabin, was viewed by the poor masses as one of their own, rather than a patrician like former presidents.

To stir up popular enthusiasm for his election, his supporters organized a kind of political carnival at which the man in the street could enjoy himself. High-spirited celebrations similar to the New Orleans Mardi Gras made politics suddenly fun, inducing millions of Americans to participate for the joy of it. Bands played, citizens danced and pranced along with them, banners waved, and elaborate floats rolled by with raised hickory poles to symbolize "Old Hickory" Jackson.

There were by then twice as many eligible voters as when Madison had been elected only 20 years earlier, because of the opening of the West and the elimination of property requirements. This vast increase in the "common man" vote gave Jackson a smashing 68 percent victory in the Electoral College. To dramatize the new spirit of democracy in the White House, Jackson rode to his inauguration on horseback.

All Americans who wanted to were invited to attend. They stormed into Washington by the thousands, crashing the White House reception. Standing on costly damask-covered chairs with muddy boots, they cheered their hero enthusiastically. Many rushed forward to pump his hand, elbowing aside the rich and fashionable. People shoved, scrambled, fought, romped. Women fainted; men got bloody noses; clothing was torn; expensive glass and china went splintering against walls and floors. A dazed Daniel Webster stammered, "I never saw anything like it!"

One Washington society woman, Margaret Bayard Smith, wrote in outrage, "What a pity what a pity! . . . The whole house had been inundated by the rabble mob. . . . The President, after having been *literally* pressed to death and almost suffocated and torn to pieces in their eagerness to shake hands with Old Hickory, had retreated through the back way and had escaped to his lodgings. . . . Those who got in could not get out by the door again, but had to scramble out of windows."

The mobs were finally lured out of the White House by tubs of punch planted on the front lawn for 20,000 people. There has never been an election celebration quite like it since.

Popular prejudice against the rich and powerful became the emotional stock-in-trade of Jackson, around whom a new Democratic party rallied. The Democrats insisted upon the rights of workers to organize, called for a ten-hour limit to the workday, demanded protection for religious minorities, championed total freedom of expression, and pressed for a secret ballot, which was already the practice in far-off Australia.

After Jackson's election, campaign hoopla and political conventions became the established procedure for nominating party candidates.

Only during Jackson's first try for the presidency in 1824, when he lost to Adams, was the popular vote first recorded. We have no idea how many Americans voted for Washington, John Adams, Jefferson, Madison, or Monroe. The only record we have of their elections is the Electoral College vote.

The reason for the Electoral College goes back to the Constitutional Convention in 1787. The states with small populations were suspicious of those with large populations. If a president were to be elected by popular vote, they feared, one big state like New York could outvote three small states like New Jersey, Delaware, and Georgia.

So a compromise was reached—the Electoral College. The aristocrats and the smaller states felt that this system would place the real power in the hands of well-to-do, outstanding citizens who would select the most qualified candidate in the nation for America's top job.

Although the Electoral College system has frequently been attacked as undemocratic, unfair, clumsy, and antiquated, no amendment to give Americans the power to elect the president and vice-president directly has ever succeeded. One reason is that a straight popular vote would reduce the importance of each state in presidential elections, with the smallest states losing the most power.

We began our national existence in 1789 as a flawed democracy. We permitted slavery, and slaves were not allowed to vote. Neither were many of the poor. Only the educated rich were allowed to hold office.

At the first meeting of the Electoral College, Washington was elected president with a 47.2 percent vote, topping the 34 percent vote of John Adams, who became vice-president. Although parties were not indicated on the ballots, both men were Federalists, advocates of strong national government, as opposed to Anti-Federalists, who favored state sovereignty. Both parties were listed for the first time in 1792, when Washington was reelected.

At first they were actually factions rather than organized political parties. The Federalists were mostly merchants, landowners, and bankers who supported the new Constitution. The Anti-Federalists were mostly workers, farmers, and local politicians who distrusted the Constitution, fearing that a rich man's aristocracy might replace the overthrown British crown.

Anti-Federalist Madison wanted a government that gave more power to the people. But Federalist Alexander Hamilton told him contemptuously, "Your people is a great beast."

Led by Jefferson and Madison, the Anti-Federalists became the Democratic-Republican Party, later known simply as the Democratic Party. The Federalists underwent several transformations, becoming in turn the National Republicans, the Whigs, and finally the Republican Party we know today.

Because no provisions for parties, or election contests between parties, had been made by the Constitution, candidates were chosen at first by congressional caucuses. In 1796 the first real contest between party candidates resulted in a narrow victory by incumbent Federalist John Adams over Democratic-Republican candidate Jefferson.

As originally conceived, the system called for the presidential candidate receiving the most electoral votes to be named president, and the candidate running second to become his vice-president.

The system was changed when passions flamed over the controversial 1800 elections. When Jefferson and Aaron Burr were tied in the Electoral College with 73 votes each, the election was thrown into the Federalist-dominated House of Representatives. Here, too, a deadlock developed. Finally, on the thirty-sixth ballot, Alexander Hamilton broke the deadlock by voting for Jefferson, whom he hated, because he loathed Burr as "a dangerous man who ought not to be trusted with the reins of government." Embittered at Hamilton, Burr subsequently challenged him to a duel and killed him.

To avoid any more messy elections like that, Congress changed the electoral system to have the president and vice-president voted for separately, our present system. It was also now recognized that the election was not just between candidates, but also between parties, so that it didn't make much sense to have a president of one party stuck with a political opponent as his vice-president just because he was the runner-up.

We take it for granted today that the election ballot is cast in secret, to make certain that it remains our own business for whom we vote. But in Jefferson's time there was no secret ballot. Each Electoral College or congressional voter had to get up in public and announce his preference, leaving himself open to reprisals from vindictive, politically powerful candidates. It was because Hamilton had had to vote against Burr openly that Burr was to take revenge by murdering him.

Another bizarre election took place in 1824, when a split developed in the ranks of the Democratic-Republican (Democratic) Party. That year the election process reverted to a contest among three candidates who ran without party designation—Andrew Jackson, John Quincy Adams, and Henry Clay.

This was the first election enumerating the popular vote. Although Jackson led 155,000 to Adams's 105,000, he failed to win an absolute majority of the Electoral College vote because his lead of 99 to 84 was diluted by Clay's 37 electoral votes. So again the election went to the House of Representatives.

To win, Jackson needed the votes of 13 of the 24 states then represented. But he had only 11, while Adams had 12. The crucial vote fell to New York, which was split evenly except for Congressman Steben Van Rennselaer, a rich patroon.

"The election turns on my vote," he reportedly sighed. "One vote will give Adams the majority. This is a responsibility I cannot bear. What shall I do?" He is alleged to have bent his head in silent prayer for guidance, after which, upon opening his eyes, he saw a discarded Adams ballot at his feet. Taking this as a divine sign, he supposedly picked it up and dropped it into the ballot box, making Adams the sixth President of the United States, despite his smaller popular vote.

One suspects, however, that a wealthy land baron who kept 100,000 tenant farmers in feudal serfdom did not really require divine guidance to persuade him to vote against Jackson, the champion of the common man.

Women were beginning to grow irked at being excluded from the electoral process under the pretext that they couldn't understand politics. Suffragettes began to protest against their second-class citizenship. In 1848 Elizabeth Cady Stanton issued a call for a Women's Rights Convention. Held at Seneca Falls, N.Y., it was the first public demand for female suffrage.

When Congress was still turning a deaf ear in 1870, Virginia Claflin Woodhull, publisher of a news weekly, warned that she intended to lead an open revolution. "We mean treason," she threatened. "We mean secession. . . . We will overthrow this bogus Republic!" Jailed, she ran unsuccessfully for president from prison as head of the Equal Rights Party against Ulysses S. Grant.

Not until almost half a century later, in 1920, were women finally granted the same right to cast ballots in American elections that men had enjoyed since the days of the Pilgrims.

By the election year of 1852, issues of slavery and expansionism had begun to divide and weaken both the Democrats and the Whigs. New parties sprang up to challenge both—principally the Republican Party and the American or Know-Nothing Party, so called because members were taught to reply, "I know nothing," when asked about its violent tactics.

The Republicans absorbed and replaced the Whigs in the 1856 elections, and four years later they nominated Abraham Lincoln as their presidential candidate. The Democrats split over the slavery issue, the South and North each fielding its own candidate. The combined Democratic vote of over 2 million outpolled Lincoln's 1,865,000. But because it was split between Stephen Douglas and John C. Breckinridge, Lincoln won his rendezvous with history.

Lincoln's conduct of the Civil War split the Republican Party. One wing, called the National Union Party, nominated him for reelection, with the support of War Democrats. The election of 1864 was the first and last in which not all the states participated—the missing eleven being the seceded Southern states, whose 81 electoral college votes were not cast.

After the war a controversy arose over whether freed slaves in the South should be permitted to vote. President Andrew Johnson was firmly opposed, claiming that this would provoke racial conflict and that the right to vote was subject to state laws. Johnson privately feared that politically active Southern blacks might sharply reduce white power.

It was President Ulysses S. Grant who won ratification of the Fifteenth Amendment, giving blacks the vote, and who executed the Enforcement Act of 1870 to empower it.

The election of 1872 developed an issue that has been controversial ever since. Under Grant the Republican Party split badly when its liberal wing, the Radical Republicans, attacked the administration for seeking to grab Santo Domingo. Feeling they could not support Grant for a second term, they ran their own candidate for president.

Party regulars denounced them as traitors, citing Stephen Decatur's famous toast: "My country, right or wrong!"

Senator Carl Schurz replied, "Our country, right or wrong! When right, to be kept right; when wrong, to be put right!"

Federalist Alexander Hamilton voted in 1800 for the Democratic-Republican candidate and his longtime adversary, Thomas Jefferson, to break the electoral college tie, thus helping to defeat Aaron Burr. ENGRAVING BY A. CHOPPEL, 1861.

REPUBLICAN
ANTI-CAUCUS TICKET.
For President,
JOHN QUINCY ADAMS,
For
VICE-PRESIDENT,
Some tried and approved Patriot.

TICKET.
Col. Stephen Wright, *Norfolk.*
Dr. Henry W. Holleman, *Surry.*
Dr. John W. King, *Dinwiddie.*
Edward R. Chambers, *Lunenburg.*
Col. John Clarke, *Halifax.*
Benjamin Hatcher, *Manchester.*
Col. William B. Lynch, *Lynchburg.*
Col. James Callaway, *Franklin.*
John M. Martin, *Nelson.*
William B. Randolph, *Henrico.*
Philip Harrison, *Fredericksburg.*
Christopher Tompkins, *Mathews.*
Robert Lively, *Hampton.*
Hancock Eustace, *Stafford.*
John Shackleford, *Culpeper.*
Capt. John P. Duval, *Fauquier.*
John Rose, *Leesburg.*
Hon. Hugh Holmes, *Winchester.*
Col. Jacob Vanmeter, *Hardy.*
Thomas J. Stuart, *Staunton.*
Pere B. Wethered, *Greenbrier.*
Peter Mayo, *Abingdon.*
Enos Thomas, *Mason.*
John S. Barnes, *Monongalia.*

In 1824, John Quincy Adams was elected president, despite his trailing in the popular vote, with 105,000 to Andrew Jackson's 155,000. This was Adams's election ballot. WOODCUT.

Elizabeth Cady Stanton initiated the first public demand for women's suffrage in 1848.

Those clashing viewpoints were to be echoed all through that century and our own, whenever the United States became enmeshed in wars, hot or cold.

One of our most questionable elections took place in 1876 between Republican Rutherford B. Hayes and Democratic Samuel J. Tilden. When the popular votes were counted, Tilden had some 250,000 more than Hayes, who went to bed resigned to having lost the election. But in the morning the Republicans refused to concede. They charged that Tilden had been unfairly elected in Louisiana, South Carolina, and Florida, because blacks had been prevented from voting in those states.

Republican leaders met in secret with Southern Democrats to strike a deal. The three contested Southern states agreed to switch their electoral votes to Hayes, in exchange for a Republican promise to withdraw federal troops from the South and let the Southern states control their own affairs. Hayes was then awarded the presidency by one electoral vote.

The Democrats roared their rage over the stolen election. Some threatened armed violence and a march on Washington to force Tilden's inauguration. Congress hastily set up an electoral commission made up of seven Democrats, seven Republicans, and one ostensibly impartial Supreme Court justice, to decide whether the Electoral College vote was valid.

Just 56 hours before Tilden had expected to be inaugurated as the nineteenth president, the commission voted 8 to 7 to accept the rigged electoral vote that had reversed the popular vote. It later turned out that the "impartial" justice on the commission had secretly been a Republican.

The election that made Benjamin Harrison president in 1888 was equally dubious. Republican politicians bought the votes they needed to win in Harrison's own Indiana, a key state. In New York they bribed the corrupt Democratic politicians of Tammany Hall, the political organization built by Aaron Burr, to fix the vote count in favor of Harrison. Even so, Grover Cleveland, the Democratic incumbent, won 100,000 more popular votes than the Republican contender. The Republicans nevertheless maneuvered to get Harrison 233 electoral votes to Cleveland's 168.

"Providence," Harrison piously told Republican National Committee Chairman Mat Quay, "has given us the victory."

Quay later laughed to a fellow politician, "Think of the man! He ought to know that Providence hadn't a damn thing to do with it!"

The 1896 presidential campaign became famous for a speech made at the Democratic National Convention by Nebraska Senator William Jennings Bryan. He led a Western demand for the free and unlimited coinage of silver, in opposition to Republican William McKinley, who favored the gold standard exclusively. What was at stake were the interests of Eastern creditors—chiefly the banks—against Western and Southern debtors, chiefly farmers. Silver was worth much less than gold. If debtors could pay off what they owed in silver instead of gold-backed currency, they could save themselves huge sums.

At the end of an impassioned speech, Bryan thundered, "You shall not press down upon the brow of labor this crown of thorns, you shall not crucify mankind upon a cross of gold!" His "Cross of Gold" speech took the Democratic convention by storm, and he was nominated its candidate for president.

Bryan traveled 13,000 miles by rail in 14 weeks, making 600 speeches in 29 states. The Republicans portrayed him as an "anarchist" and "revolutionist." McKinley, who disdained campaigning as undignified, stayed home and from his front porch addressed state delegations brought to him by train.

Bryan lost the election. But ever since, "dark-horse" candidates for the presidency have hoped to emulate his example by sweeping convention delegates off their feet with a brilliant speech, winning the nomination by acclaim.

States varied in the methods they preferred for choosing delegates to the national party conventions that would select candidates. In one state, delegates of the victorious party would be pledged to vote for one particular presidential candidate. In another, elected delegates supporting a candidate would still be left free to make up their own minds at the convention. Such delegations were often split in their choices, rather than voting as a solid bloc. This difference is still valid today.

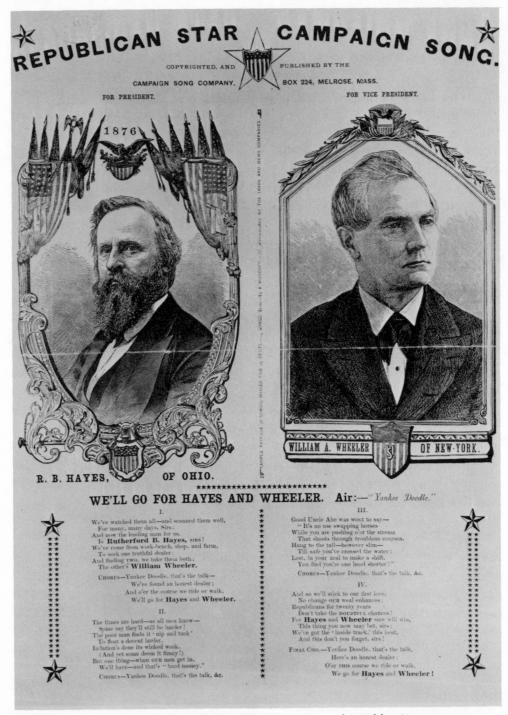

Republican Rutherford B. Hayes defeated Democrat Samuel J. Tilden in a controversial "stolen" presidential election in 1876. This was Hayes's campaign song. WOODCUT PUBLISHED BY THE CAMPAIGN SONG COMPANY, COPYRIGHT 1876.

This drawing shows the crowd outside the New York Herald office on election night in 1860, reading the returns. WOOD ENGRAVING IN HARPER'S WEEKLY, NOVEMBER 1860.

This 1896 Washington Post cartoon shows William Jennings Bryan, dark horse of the Democratic convention with his "Cross of Gold" speech. PEN AND INK DRAWING BY G. Y. COFFIN, AUGUST 1896.

The election campaign of 1928 between Democrat Al Smith and Republican Herbert Hoover was significant for the issues involved. The first Roman Catholic to run for the White House, Smith was subjected to a vicious anti-Catholic campaign that insisted his victory would give the Pope a "pipeline to the White House." Another key issue was Smith's stand that Prohibition, the Eighteenth Amendment which had given rise to speakeasies and gangster warfare to control the illicit liquor trade, should be repealed as a failed experiment.

The Democratic platform also pledged collective bargaining for labor and federal relief for hard-pressed farmers. Hoover branded this program "state socialism," insisting that "rugged individualism" was the traditional American way.

This contest, which Smith lost, sharpened the issues between Democrats and Republicans. It foreshadowed the confrontation between Hoover and Franklin Delano Roosevelt four years later in the depths of the Great Depression.

Roosevelt, confined to a wheelchair because of polio, nevertheless campaigned vigorously, covering 27,000 miles in 41 states. Addressing 14 million unemployed Americans, he promised them a "New Deal." Hoover accused Roosevelt of prescribing communism for the United States, and he warned that a Democratic victory would mean "grass will grow in the streets of a hundred cities." But Roosevelt won by a landslide of over 7 million votes, carrying 42 out of the 48 states.

Then in 1936 he won reelection easily, and in 1940 he broke precedent by running for a third time. The Republicans screamed foul and ran a Republican liberal against him. The Democrats reelected Roosevelt with the slogan: "Better a third termer than a third rater!" Roosevelt was so popular during World War II that he easily won a fourth term as well, but he died less than three months into it. No president before or since was ever elected to more than two terms.

When the Republicans sought to win the White House away from his successor, Harry S Truman, in 1952, they drafted as their candidate Dwight D. ("Ike") Eisenhower, a popular military hero of World War II. Eisenhower was irked by the Republican National Committee, complaining, "All they talked about was how they should win on my popularity. Nobody said I had a brain in my head!" Personality was the magic ingredient.

The Democratic Convention nominated the witty governor of Illinois, Adlai Stevenson, as their candidate. Eisenhower's friend George Allen assured him, "Stevenson will be easy to beat. He's too accomplished an orator!"

The history of our elections has largely validated Allen's assessment. Intellectuals seldom win the White House, with the notable exceptions of Thomas Jefferson and Woodrow Wilson. Most Americans do not identify with brainy candidates, feeling more comfortable with conventional or ordinary types.

The Eisenhower-Stevenson contest was the first in which TV was an important campaign tool. Actor Robert Montgomery directed Eisenhower's TV appearances. Americans were captivated by the candidate's engaging charm and warmth. They saw him as a candid, modest, "typical American nice guy," a kindly father figure who would keep the nation safe and secure in peace, as he had in war. In contrast, viewers saw the sophisticated Stevenson as a college professor with "more brains than heart."

"I Like Ike" buttons sprouted on millions of coat lapels and dresses. By campaigning as himself, rather than as the Republican candidate, Eisenhower made it possible for millions of Democrats to split their ticket and vote for him personally, while voting for Democrats in all other offices.

"Democrats for Eisenhower" clubs sprang up all over the South. When he spoke at Harvard, his car was mobbed by collegiate souvenir hunters. Police had to make a solid shield of their bodies to keep admirers from tearing off his clothes and "at times," he sighed, "I thought even part of my arm!"

Eisenhower won a stunning victory—the first Republican presidential win in 24 years—with almost 7 million more votes than Stevenson and over 86 percent of the Electoral College vote.

After his second term, Vice-President Richard M. Nixon sought to succeed him. The Democrats' candidate was John F. Kennedy. The contest was basically decided by a series of four TV debates held in September and October of 1960, the first time TV had ever played a decisive role in determining the presidency. Before an audience of up to 70 million Americans, a confident, vigorous Kennedy triumphed over the sallow, nervous Nixon, who blamed his TV image for his defeat.

Seeking a political comeback two years later, Nixon raced Edmund G. Brown for the governorship of California. Losing, he told news reporters bitterly, "Well, you won't have Richard Nixon to kick around any more!" This added to his political handicap the reputation of being a sore loser.

When President Kennedy was assassinated in 1963, he was succeeded by Vice-President Lyndon Johnson, who won a term of his own the following year. Involving the United States deeply in the unpopular Vietnam War, Johnson promised voters that he had no intention of sending "American boys 9,000 or 10,000 miles away from home to do what Asian boys ought to be doing for themselves." But he ended up sending half a million U.S. troops to do just that, angering some supporters who thought he was neglecting his promise to build a "Great Society" at home to help poor and black Americans.

Anti-war and anti-draft demonstrations erupted all across America. Along with ghetto riots, civil disorders, student revolts, and a people's march on Washington, they forced Johnson to realize that he could not be reelected. So in 1968 he threw his weight behind the candidacy of his vice-president, Hubert Humphrey, who promised to persist with the Vietnam War.

Meanwhile Senator Robert Kennedy, brother of the assassinated president, entered state Democratic primaries as a presidential candidate. When Humphrey announced that he would campaign with "the politics of joy," Kennedy told crowds, "If you want to be filled with pablum and tranquilizers, then don't vote for me. . . . If you see a small black child starving to death in the Mississippi delta, as I have, you know this is not the politics of joy. I'm not going to be like that."

He accused the Johnson administration of spending $300,000 per Vietnamese soldier killed, while millions of poor Americans went to bed hungry every night. His campaign was so successful that it looked as though a second Kennedy would go to the White House. But just as he won the important California primary, he fell to an assassin's bullet, just like his brother. His death cleared the way for the Democratic nomination of Humphrey.

But anti-war Democrats staged stormy street demonstrations against that nomination at the Democratic National Convention in Chicago. They demanded the nomination of Senator Eugene McCarthy of Minnesota, who promised to end the Vietnam War. The Chicago police of Mayor Richard J. Daley, a Johnson/Humphrey loyalist, rushed out in force to break up the demonstrations violently. In bloody clashes, young dissenters were beaten, subjected to tear gas and Mace, and dragged into police vans. TV cameramen filming these scenes were also attacked by police. Indignant delegates inside the convention hall angrily denouncd Mayor Daley for using "gestapo tactics." An impartial presidential commission investigating these election disorders later called them "a police riot." But the Johnson forces were able to ram through Humphrey's nomination.

Meanwhile Richard Nixon, shaking off the "Tricky Dickie" image that had plagued him as a public figure, campaigned for the Republican nomination. He cinched it by a "Southern strategy" that pledged to downplay school integration and civil rights programs, in return for the support of leading Southern Republicans. The program was also designed to win over conservative Southern Democrats, known as "Boll Weevils," in the general election.

His strategy radically changed the electoral picture in the United States. Since the days of the Civil War, white Southerners had punished Abraham Lincoln's Republican Party by persistently voting Democratic. But in 1968 this pattern fragmented. Millions of traditional Democrats either went over to Nixon or voted for Democratic Governor George Wallace of Alabama, who bolted his party to head a new American Independent Party opposed to civil rights.

At the Republican convention, Nixon was nominated over rivals Ronald Reagan and New York Governor Nelson Rockefeller. To reward his Southern supporters, he took Maryland's Governor Spiro T. Agnew as his running mate. He campaigned with promises to end the Vietnam War, negotiate with the communist powers, and restore "law and order" to the turbulent streets of America.

Humphrey's problems were compounded by the disgust of Democratic liberals with the violence at the Chicago convention and with his pledge to continue the Vietnam War. Millions stayed away from the polls or voted a third-party ticket in protest. Nixon won the election.

He soon infuriated young Americans, especially those on college campuses, by intensifying the Vietnam War instead of ending it as he had promised. Anti-war rallies swept the country as Nixon appealed to America's "silent majority" to support him. When over half a million people marched in a Washington protest, Nixon ordered the Justice Department to make mass arrests. The 13,400 arrests were afterward declared illegal. When six students were killed by National Guardsmen in Kent State, Ohio, and Jackson State, Mississippi, college demonstrations, over 440 campuses shut down in a national protest strike.

Nervous about his chances for reelection, Nixon's aides sent a burglary squad into Democratic offices in the Watergate complex in Washington to steal campaign secrets. The burglars were caught red-handed. When their links to the White House were exposed by two reporters of the *Washington Post*, the president and his top aides tried to conceal their responsibility for this and other election campaign misdeeds.

Their cover-up succeeded well enough to let Nixon win reelection in 1972 over liberal Democratic candidate George McGovern. The Nixon campaign violated many provisions of the Federal Election Campaign Act of 1971, which set limits to the sources and spending of campaign funds. Through their Committee to Reelect the President (CRP), the Nixon forces secretly raised and spent huge sums illegally, in part for a "department of dirty tricks."

When these facts and the president's guilt in the Watergate cover-up were exposed early in his second term, Nixon was faced with impeachment by Congress and was forced to resign. Before doing so, he had forced the resignation of Vice-President Agnew, who was facing prosecution for previous crimes in Maryland. Nixon named Representative Gerald Ford of Michigan as the new Vice-President. When Ford replaced Nixon in the White House, he protected Nixon from prosecution for his misdeeds by issuing him a pardon.

The election of 1976 pitted Ford against Democratic Governor Jimmy Carter of Georgia. Carter won the White House by a narrow one percent of the popular vote. He was defeated after only one term, partly because of his failure to obtain the release of 52 American hostages held in Iran after a revolution. Republican Ronald Reagan's landslide victory also gave the Republicans control of the Senate and a working arrangement with conservative Southern Democrats ("Boll Weevils") in the House of Representatives.

The Reagan victory demonstrated the remarkable resilience of the American political system. After the Republicans' Watergate disaster, political experts predicted that they were finished as a party. Yet only six years later they were back in power, even though most registered voters were Democrats.

6

WHAT IT TAKES
TO BE A CANDIDATE

The word "candidate" comes from the Latin *candidatus*, meaning "clothed in white." In ancient Rome, candidates for the Roman Senate had to appear in public places draped only in a white "gown of humility," which they had to lift upon request to show their war wounds, proof of their service to Rome.

In Shakespeare's play *Coriolanus*, that proud Roman warrior wants to be elected consul, but he begs the Senators, "I do beseech you, let me o'erleap that custom, for I cannot put on the gown, stand naked, and entreat them, for my wounds' sake, to give their suffrage."

In the United States today, candidates must come before the public and display their qualifications to the voters whose favor they seek. Aspirants for the White House must be at least 35, native-born citizens, and residents of the nation for at least 14 years. Our youngest presidents when they assumed office were Theodore Roosevelt, at 42, and John F. Kennedy, at 43; our oldest, Ronald Reagan, at 69.

Most Americans expect presidential candidates to seek the office actively, but out of a desire to serve the nation rather than out of personal ambition; to be experienced in some high government office; to have a pleasing personality; to have leadership quality and skilled persuasive powers.

Bearing a famous name can help. Franklin D. Roosevelt was no national figure when he ran for the White House in 1932. But the name of his distant cousin, former President Teddy Roosevelt, didn't hurt. "One of my best political assets," he said, "is that a lot of backcountry folks think I'm Theodore!"

White, Anglo-Saxon, Protestant (WASP), male candidates stand the best chance of nomination and election, because they represent the stereotype of leadership to American voters. Nevertheless we have already had one Catholic president, whose brother Robert Kennedy declared in 1961, "There is no question about it. In the next forty years a Negro can achieve the same position my brother has." In 1983 black leader Jesse Jackson challenged the Democratic Party to nominate a black for president in 1984, and then announced his own candidacy.

Black candidates for Mayor had already been elected in seven major American cities—Los Angeles, Detroit, Atlanta, Washington, New Orleans, Newark, and Chicago.

A presidential candidate's personal life must be able to withstand intense scrutiny. Voters prefer family men who have not been divorced, although their divorces did not prevent Adlai Stevenson from becoming the Democratic candidate in 1952 and 1956, nor Reagan from becoming president in 1980.

If a candidate is not well-known, he faces an uphill battle to win media attention. When Jimmy Carter, former governor of Georgia, announced his candidacy, even his hometown newspaper ridiculed him by headlining the story: "Jimmy *Who* Is Running for *What*?" The "Jimmy Who?" tag plagued him through much of his campaign. But Carter plunged doggedly ahead, talking to people in shopping centers and supermarkets and at Democratic dinners, winning state primary after primary until the media were forced to take notice.

The candidate considered the "front-runner" for his party's presidential nomination is usually the one who emerges first in public-opinion polls and state primaries. The front-runner has the advantage of getting most media attention and of attracting campaign funds. The disadvantage is that in the white-hot glare of publicity, any mistake he makes is magnified, and the loss of any state primary may destroy his image as a winner.

In 1974 Senator Walter Mondale decided not to compete with Jimmy

Carter for the 1976 Democratic nomination, stating, "I found that I did not have the overwhelming desire to be president." He did not, he explained, want to spend two years of his life living in Holiday Inns on the campaign trail. But it's the rare politician who resists the temptation of America's top office when opportunity knocks. After serving as Carter's vice-president, Mondale changed his mind and became an active campaigner for the Democratic nomination in 1984.

A candidate needs to be perceived to have good physical and mental health to stand up to the strains of the Oval Office. The remarkable exception to this rule was Franklin D. Roosevelt, elected four times despite being in a wheelchair, disabled by polio. He had spent two years in bed just trying to move his big toe, after which, he said, "anything else seems easy."

Sturdy physical health was actually more important for a president in the old days, when Washington was built on a partially reclaimed marshland infested with mosquitoes, malarial fever, rats, and bad drinking water.

Character is invariably considered more important than intelligence by most voters. Adlai Stevenson was a brilliant candidate; his campaign speeches were witty, original, and brainy. In contrast, Dwight Eisenhower was a dull, uninspired speaker. But Republicans pinned the label of "egghead" on Stevenson, suggesting he was not practical enough to be trusted with the presidency, and Stevenson lost twice to Eisenhower.

Most candidates for the White House, and for Congress, are lawyers—some 60 percent of all presidents, about 67 percent of senators, and 53 percent of representatives. There is some justification for it. Lawyers are familiar with the operations of the law, which is what government is all about. They are also trained to be persuasive public speakers. Familiar with the business world, they often have as clients wealthy men who can provide them with campaign funds.

The next most frequent occupation of those who seek public office is that of businessman. In earlier times military heroes like George Washington were sought as presidential candidates, because of the awe in which they were held by unsophisticated Americans. Andrew Jackson and William Harrison, for example, were considered presidential caliber because of their prowess as Indian fighters.

Through determined personal campaigning, Jimmy Carter fought inattention by the media, to become president in 1976.

Ronald Reagan was elected president in 1980, the oldest man elected to that office. He was 69 at the time.

Ulysses S. Grant had little to recommend him except his renown as the general who had won the Civil War. When scandals broke out under his administration, he admitted sadly, "It was my fortune, or misfortune, to be called to the office of the Chief Executive without any previous political training."

Civil War General William Tecumseh Sherman commented acidly on the naiveté of Americans in believing that because a man was expert at the science of killing, he therefore possessed the necessary civilian skills to govern the nation. "Any senator," he insisted, "can step from his chair at the Capitol into the White House, and fulfill the office of president with more skill and success than a Grant, Sherman, or Sheridan who . . . were not schooled in the practice by which civil communities are and should be governed."

Confederate General Robert E. Lee also mused on the failure of most Army men in public life: "It is rare that any one of them have achieved success." Even Dwight Eisenhower declared, four years before he gave up his general's stars for the Oval Office, "The necessary and wise subordination of the military to civil power will be best sustained when lifelong professional soldiers abstain from seeking high political office."

When Eisenhower was persuaded to seek the presidency, President Truman grinned. "He'll sit here, and he'll say, 'Do this! Do that!' And nothing will happen. Poor Ike—it won't be a bit like the Army. He'll find it very frustrating."

Today no political party risks nominating a military man as its presidential candidate. Too many voters have become wary of the military mind, especially with the grave risk of precipitating a nuclear war.

Candidates who aspire to the White House have to spend years in advance of their party's nominating convention trying to win support. They have to travel thousands of miles from state to state wooing party leaders. Standing in front of stores and factory gates, they have to shake hands and kiss babies. They have to speak to every group that will listen, attend fairs, give away bumper stickers and buttons, get on radio and TV programs, attend organization dinners, and often end each day on the campaign trail totally exhausted.

Yet when William Henry Harrison addressed a campaign meeting in 1840, he said, "It has ever appeared to me that the office of the President of the United States should not be sought after by any individual, but that the people should spontaneously, and with their own free will, accord the distinguishing honor to the man whom they believed would best perform its important duties."

Similarly, when William McKinley sought the Republican nomination in 1896, he refused to leave home to seek it. "I cannot get the consent of my mind," he declared, "to do anything that places me in the position of seeming to seek an office."

President Harry S Truman disagreed emphatically. "This draft business is hooey," he scoffed. "There never was a man drafted for president in the history of the country. A draft is created by the fellow who wants it and is willing to fight for it."

The president in office who wants a second term has a distinct advantage over all challengers in his party. He is seldom denied renomination. Even party members dissatisfied with him will vote for him again if it appears that he offers the best chance of defeating the opposition.

Abraham Lincoln's conduct of the Civil War angered many of his own party, who wanted to deny him renomination. Horace Greeley, the influential editor who had originally supported him, wrote: "Mr. Lincoln is already beaten. He cannot be elected. We must have another ticket to save us from utter overthrow." But many Republicans felt that to deny Lincoln renomination would be an admission that their war policy had been a mistake. "Don't swap horses in midstream!" they urged.

Lincoln won another term to finish the war.

It helps a candidate's chances if he comes from a state with a big population, since he is assumed to have a good chance to command that important bloc of votes.

He is also expected to look "presidential"—dignified, powerful, imposing, tall, assured, photogenic. "I think the American public wants a solemn ass as president," wryly observed President Calvin Coolidge. Perhaps the most presidential-looking president ever to occupy the White House was Warren G. Harding, who turned out to be one of the worst of our chief executives, presiding over a corrupt, inefficient administration riddled with scandal.

Nevertheless there is no denying the impact on voters of a candidate's appearance. This was highlighted in the race between Richard M. Nixon and John F. Kennedy in 1960. When Nixon agreed to a series of

TV debates with Kennedy, they were watched by over 120 million Americans. Kennedy projected the image of a handsome, intelligent, well informed, clean-cut young leader. Nixon seemed unattractive, awkward, and malevolent. These contrasting images, probably more than anything the two candidates said, decided the election.

When California's sixty-eight-year-old Senator Alan Cranston sought the 1984 Democratic presidential nomination, he was criticized for being bald, unglamorous, and too old. One constituent, Elise Beraru of Los Angeles, wrote *Newsweek* angrily, "Our insistence that our presidential candidates be 'pretty' rather than effective will condemn us forever to the Jimmy Carters and Ronald Reagans who populate American politics."

Tact is an important attribute for a candidate; without it he may get himself in hot water with large groups of voters. Jefferson lost urban votes by declaring wryly, "The mobs of the great cities add just as much to the support of pure government as sores do to the support of the human body."

When Theodore Roosevelt castigated anti-war Americans as "undesirable citizens," over a million voters promptly pinned on buttons proclaiming, "I'm an undesirable citizen."

When Wilson ran for president, his rivals circulated earlier writings in which he had expressed contempt for "sordid" Polish, Hungarian, and Italian immigrants as a "coarse crew." Wilson had to apologize to spokesmen for these groups.

Adlai Stevenson once joked that a politician was a statesman who approached every question with an open mouth.

A prime concern of every candidate is how to win time and space from the media. In ancient Rome a candidate's supporter would paint notices about him on walls. Modern campaign managers leave no stone unturned to get their candidates a constant stream of favorable publicity.

How the media portray candidates has tremendous impact on how voters perceive them. Voters are often alienated by candidates represented as racists, radical leftists, extreme right-wingers, lamebrains, warmongers, big business apologists, cronies of labor racketeers, or anti-conservationists.

Candidates who rank high in the public-opinion polls tend to receive more media attention than those who do not. Likewise, those who receive more media attention tend to rank high in the polls. This closed circle makes it difficult for new faces to win serious consideration as candidates. It is also difficult for them to raise adequate funds for their campaigns, since they are considered long shots. Contributors prefer to bet on favorites to win.

"We have put a dollar sign on public service," declared President Eisenhower, "and today many capable men who would like to run for office simply can't afford to do so. Many believe that politics in our country is already a game exclusively for the affluent. This is not strictly true; yet the fact that we may be approaching that state of affairs is a sad reflection on our elective system."

Eisenhower himself had to raise $4 million for his own campaign in 1952. One problem with such fund raising is that the candidate incurs obligations to the persons who help him raise the funds. Eisenhower's finance committee was headed by New York banker Winthrop W. Aldrich. Within weeks after Eisenhower entered the White House, Aldrich was appointed to the choice post of Ambassador to Britain. Democratic presidents have also rewarded their fund raisers with important appointments.

Often rich men themselves become candidates for public office, spending small fortunes to get elected, primarily to enjoy the prestige and power. Nelson Rockefeller, for example, spent over $5 million in 1966 to get elected to the $50,000-a-year job of governor of New York. The Supreme Court has ruled that wealthy candidates cannot be prevented from spending as much of their own money as they want on their own campaigns, calling this a form of "free expression."

The total amount spent by all candidates in the 1980 national elections broke the billion-dollar mark for the first time, doubling the amount spent in 1976. In his book *Financing the 1980 Election*, Professor Herbert Alexander blames the increasing use of costly high technology—computers, opinion polls, direct mail, and wildly expensive TV advertising.

The Federal Election Commission also reported that candidates running for Congress in the off-year elections of 1982 spent more money than in any past Congressional elections. Senate candidates spent an average of almost $2 million apiece, and House candidates an average of over $200,000 each.

Victory can nevertheless elude the candidate with the biggest campaign fund. In 1982, Mark Dayton of Minnesota spent $7.2 million, much of it his own money, seeking a Senate seat, only to lose to incumbent David Durenberger, who spent less than $4 million.

In 1972 the dairy industry donated $2 million to President Nixon's reelection campaign, in return for a promised increase in milk price supports. When this and similar deals surfaced in 1974, a shocked Congress passed amendments to the Federal Election Campaigns Act that limited organizations to a maximum contribution of $5,000 per candidate and individuals to a maximum $1,000 contribution per candidate. Public disclosure had to be made for all large contributions.

To lessen the need for candidates to obligate themselves to private supporters, the major parties were offered $2 million apiece in public funds for their national convention and up to $20 million each during a presidential election, provided they agreed to forego private financing.

Candidates have been able to circumvent all limitations, however, by the use of Political Action Committees (PACs), which ostensibly operate in their behalf but outside their control. These clubs are set up by business, labor unions, and other special-interest groups to further the campaigns of candidates of their choice. The PAC campaigns are in addition to, and independent of, the candidates' official campaigns.

The Republicans, generally favored by big business, have always been able to raise much more money than the Democrats. In the 1980 presidential election, Ronald Reagan's campaign expenditures were six times greater than Jimmy Carter's. Nevertheless, from 1932 through 1980, the Democrats still won 8 of the 13 presidential contests.

Colorado Senator Gary Hart, who managed the presidential campaign of Senator George McGovern in 1972, explained how the nomination of a candidate is achieved: "You start out with small meetings. Then you go on to the next circle using that network to reach several thousand people. You ask them to reach out, hopefully, to tens of thousands of people. This is a long, long process." He estimated that candidates have to spend up to half their time soliciting campaign funds.

Democratic candidate John Glenn sighed in 1983, "I'd rather rassle a gorilla on the floor than ask somebody for 50 cents." But the higher the office to which a candidate aspires, the more money he needs to mount a credible campaign.

A presidential candidate also needs a thick skin. He must be able to take criticism and verbal abuse, much of it unfair, by rivals and the media. Should he win the White House, he must still expect further abuse from segments of the country that remain opposed to him.

When Lincoln was president, even in the North he was vilified as a drunkard, atheist, socialist, and baboon. *Harper's Weekly* described him as "a Filthy Story-Teller, Despot, Liar, Thief, Braggart, Buffoon, Usurper, Monster, Ignoramus Abe, Old Scoundrel, Perjurer, Robber, Swindler, Tyrant, Fiend, Butcher, Land-Pirate."

But as President Truman once suggested, "If you can't stand the heat, stay out of the kitchen."

A sense of humor helps. Representative Morris K. Udall of Arizona tells of campaigning in New Hampshire in 1976 and approaching two men who were whittling. "Mo Udall, running for president," he introduced himself. One replied dryly, "Yep, we know. We were just laughing about it."

Presidential candidates also need to be free of any breath of scandal in their past. In 1969 Senator Edward Kennedy became involved in a tragic accident when a car he was driving on Chappaquiddick Island, Massachusetts, plunged off a bridge and into a tidal pool, drowning a female aide. Kennedy's account of his role in the accident aroused considerable skepticism. Subsequently, whenever the prospect of his presidential candidacy came up, the Democrats hesitated to nominate him, for fear the Republicans and the media would continually remind voters of Chappaquiddick.

A "dark-horse" candidate is one given only an outside chance of winning his party's nomination. He hopes that if the front-runner and other top candidates fail to muster enough votes, the convention might then turn to him as a compromise candidate acceptable to all and opposed by few. This was how Lincoln won the Republican nomination in 1860.

"My name is new in the field," he wrote to a supporter, "and I suppose I am not the first choice of a great many. Our policy, then, is to give no offense to others—leave them in a mood to come to us if they shall be compelled to give up their first love."

Candidates and their campaign managers need to be skillful at wheeling and dealing in political conventions. They often have to persuade delegates in opposition to change camps, while holding onto their own pledged delegates against similar raids by their rivals. They may promise rewards or hint at reprisals in order to round up the votes they need.

It has not escaped women that no major party has ever nominated a woman as its candidate for president or vice-president. Professional politicians insist that the vast majority of American voters aren't ready for that innovation.

Nevertheless in 1972 at the Democratic National Convention, Representative Shirley Chisholm of New York became a candidate for the presidential nomination, and Frances Farenthold of Texas sought the vice-presidential nomination.

"Many women now see that a career and family are not mutually exclusive for them any more than . . . for a man," declares Susanne Paizis in her book *Getting Her Elected*. "Many more women are eager to participate in government. . . . Little girls can grow up wanting to be president just like little boys do. And one day, one of them *will* be president."

Meanwhile, feminists are urging more and more women to run for Congress to demonstrate female ability in seats of power. "A woman's place is in the House," one woman politician rewrote the old bromide, "and also in the Senate!"

The decade of the 1970's seemed to mark an important turning point for women in politics. Many communities voted for their first woman mayor, town councilor, county commissioner, state representative, lieutenant governor, governor, congressperson, and senator.

"I think one of my major uses," said Shirley Chisholm, "is as an example to the women of our country, to show them that if a woman has ability, stamina, organizational skill, and a knowledge of the issues, she can win public office."

The National Women's Political Caucus, founded in 1971, played an important role in winning greater consideration and participation for women in the political process. The following year fully 40 percent of the delegates at the Democratic National Convention were women. The Republican Convention hastily increased its number of female delegates from the previous 17 percent to 30 percent. And Republican feminists were able to get a women's rights plank inserted in the party platform.

"Talented women are wasted playing supportive roles only," observed an editorial in the Macon, Georgia, *Telegraph*. It added, "Developing leadership among women, both as party workers and as elected officials, is important. . . . We need women in politics."

The nation began to see women governors—Ella Grasso in Connecticut, Dixy Lee Ray in Washington—and as many as six lieutenant governors. The number of women state legislators doubled in the ten years ending in 1979, a period which saw the election of Jane Byrne as mayor of Chicago and Dianne Feinstein as mayor of San Francisco.

When March Fong Eu became California's secretary of state, she declared, "I think none of us can deny the fact that women have traditionally found greater barriers to effective campaigning than men. We're inexperienced, and often not comfortable asking people for money, for example. Nevertheless, none of us can deny that women are entering the political field with increasing success." Dianne Feinstein, for example, became one of the first woman candidates to be considered by the Democratic Party for the office of vice-president.

In the 1980 Congressional races, almost 15 percent of the major party candidates for the Senate were women, while 51 female candidates were nominated for the House.

"There are more activists among women now," noted House Speaker Tip O'Neill. "The ERA [Equal Rights Amendment] is responsible in part. It's activated a lot of women. It's the trend that's coming."

On the other hand, Colorado Congresswoman Pat Schroeder felt that political progress for women was too slow. "We are still a novelty act," she complained in 1979. Asked by skeptics how she could effectively deal with both motherhood and her political career, she replied, "I have a brain and a uterus—and they both work."

Democratic candidate Jimmy Carter with incumbent President Gerald R. Ford on the set of their 1976 television debate. Media portrayal of candidates influences voters. PHOTO BY FRED.

THE TWO ADAMS: "IT WAS MY RIB, EVE"

Once women were granted the right to vote, they were courted by both political parties—the Democrats and the Republicans (Grand Old Party). POLITICAL CARTOON BY J. F. KNOTT IN THE DALLAS MORNING NEWS, AUGUST 29, 1920.

To become a candidate for the United States Senate, a man or woman must be at least 30, and have been a citizen for 9 years. To run for the House of Representatives, a person must be at least 25, and have been a citizen for 7 years. Both must be residents of the state represented. A senator serves for six years, a representative for two.

Because of their longer term of service and their fewer numbers, senators have a better chance than representatives of becoming well-known enough to win consideration as presidential candidates. But it costs a lot more to campaign for the Senate.

Candidates for the office of vice-president are aware that it commands little power. Vice-President John Garner, disgruntled that he was given practically nothing to do by President Franklin D. Roosevelt, groused inelegantly that the office "wa'nt worth a pitcher of warm spit."

Nevertheless, the vice-president may suddenly become president because of the death or assassination of the chief executive, as has happened a number of times. The vice-president also has a good chance to be nominated by his party as successor to the president.

Voters are often disappointed in the candidates they elect to the White House. President Truman warned Americans against regarding any candidate with starry-eyed worship, expecting him to be a super-man. When we do, we are fated to be disappointed.

Any president, Mr. Truman reminded us wryly, is only a man like the rest of us, who puts on his pants one leg at a time.

7

WHAT THE DEMOCRATS
ARE ALL ABOUT

When President Truman campaigned to remain in the Oval Office in 1948, the Republicans castigated him as a typical Democratic bureaucrat. Truman told reporters with a grin, "You know what a bureaucrat is? A bureaucrat is a Democrat who's got a job a Republican wants!"

In the early 1950's, Republican Party leaders grew annoyed by the implications of the Democratic Party name, which seemed to suggest that it was the party of democracy. Republican National Committee Chairman Leonard Hall began referring to his opponents simply as the "Democrat Party," dropping the "ic." He explained to the media, "I think their claims that they represent the great mass of people, and we don't, is just a lot of bunk!"

Democrats do like to consider themselves the party of the common people, looking out for the interests of ordinary Americans, in contrast to the Republicans, whom Democrats label the party of big business and banks.

The origins of the Democratic Party go back to the Anti-Federalists, who then became Democratic-Republicans. Those who flocked to its banners were chiefly farmers, city workers, small businessmen, and some professional people. During the Jackson administration the name was considered too unwieldy, and it was shortened to simply the Democratic Party.

The party was founded on Jefferson's belief that the government should be close to the people, serving their needs rather than the demands of powerful special interests. The Democratic program, sensitive to public hardships and geared to do for individuals what they are unable to do for themselves, has become known as *liberalism*. In practice this policy has meant unemployment insurance for the jobless, medical care for the poor who are ill, welfare for the poor who cannot work, and Social Security payments for the aged and handicapped—all measures first introduced by the Democrats.

The party tends to be a coalition of many different groups. Traditionally the Democrats have been heavily supported by minorities in the population—Catholics, Jews, blacks, union members, most Hispanics, and immigrants. These groups have tended to view the Republicans as controlling the economic power structure that excluded them, while considering the Democrats their defenders.

The Democratic Party claims credit for almost all the landmark legislation for social and economic reform. They initiated and passed the Adamson (eight-hour workday) Act, women's suffrage, TVA (federal power supplied to Tennessee Valley farms), the Wagner Act (giving union labor bargaining power against big corporations), Social Security, the Rural Electrification Act, federal housing acts, the Full Employment Act, the Low Rent Housing and Slum Clearance Act, civil rights acts (protecting minorities from discrimination and guaranteeing equal education), the Minimum Wage Act, and other important changes in our system.

Because Democratic programs have cost a great deal of money, they are often attacked by Republicans as being wasteful and a heavy burden on taxpayers. The Democratic view is that money is less important than equal opportunity for all Americans.

A basic difference between the parties is that the Democrats, who call themselves "the party of progress," favor the maximum use of the federal government to solve the nation's problems, while the Republicans want a minimum of federal involvement, calling instead upon the states and private organizations to do the job at local levels.

The Democrats' greatest voting strength is in the nation's big cities, where most minorities live and where most people have a liberal outlook. The Republicans rely more on rural and suburban areas, which tend to be conservative.

The father of our country, George Washington, was considered a conservative Federalist, but he refused to call himself one. He opposed the development of separate political parties, fearing they would destroy national unity, much as the Whigs and Tories had been at each other's throats before the Revolution. "If I could not go to heaven but with a party," Washington vowed, "I would not go there at all."

Parties were unnecessary at first because there was general agreement that Washington should be our first president. But as his second term came to an end, there was no agreement on who should succeed him. It was then that the Democratic-Republicans were formed to elect a president sympathetic to farmers and city workers. At that time the Republican part of their name signified that they opposed kings and favored the French Revolution. On the other side of the fence, the Federalists, representing bankers, businessmen, and the middle class, viewed the Democratic-Republicans distastefully as "the party of the mob."

After the Federalist regimes of Washington and John Adams, the Democrats held the White House from Jefferson's election in 1800 for 11 out of 14 presidential terms. The twenty-four-year period of the Jefferson, Madison, and Monroe administrations was known as "the era of good feeling," because there was little serious opposition to the Democratic-Republican Party.

Party platforms—the party's promises to voters—did not become a part of the election process until 1840. The Democrats wrote the first one, deciding it made sense to spell out to voters what the party's candidates stood for. Then as now, however, what parties promised to do if elected often bore little resemblance to what they actually did once having persuaded the electorate to put them in power.

Most of the early political machines that developed in the large cities were Democratic and corrupt. Editor Horace Greeley ran exposés of New York's "Bloody Sixth" ward, an almost all-Irish election district whose political bosses organized thugs to terrorize the voting booths, driving off Whig voters. The ward bosses threatened to smash Greeley's presses unless he printed a retraction. Instead he sponsored a bill to

Th. Jefferson

The election of Democratic-Republican Thomas Jefferson in 1800 began the "era of good feeling," when there was little opposition to that party for almost a quarter of a century.
WOOD ENGRAVING BY HENRY WOLF, 1901.

register voters as a method of fraud prevention, and armed his employees with muskets from the City Guard to defend the paper.

By 1855 Irish-Catholic immigrants made up 34 percent of New York City's electorate. They voted a solid Democratic ticket in gratitude to the ward bosses who helped them out of trouble and got them city jobs. Anti-Catholic prejudice was held in check by a 100 percent Irish police force, which limited the attacks by extremist Whig, American Republican, and "Known Nothing" Party mobs on the Democrats.

As Irish immigration swelled, so did the power of the Democrats in many big cities of the Northeast. In Boston one year, four Irish ward bosses met privately to dictate the city's Democratic nominations. Three opposed the grabbing of a seat in the House of Representatives by the fourth, John Francis "Honey Fitz" Fitzgerald, known as the Napoleon of the Sixth Ward.

He thwarted them by simply arming a mob of seamen with pistols, paying them to toss out of the polls all but Fitzgerald voters. Subsequently he made himself mayor of Boston. To sell city jobs to those willing to pay him for the appointments, he circumvented civil service requirements by inventing jobs like Tea Warmers, Tree Climbers, and Wipers.

Big-city voters tolerated the corrupt Democratic political machines partly out of fear and partly because of favors and services the ward bosses provided to loyal voters.

In the 1840's the Democrats put themselves in front of an aggressive new movement of expansion. As New York newspaperman John L. O'Sullivan put it, Americans had the "manifest destiny to occupy and to possess the whole of the Continent which Providence has given to us." When the Democrats elected James K. Polk to the White House, he began the Mexican War to grab the New Mexico and California territories from Mexico.

General Lewis Cass of Michigan won the Democratic nomination to succeed Polk, advocating further annexations for the "glory of the nation." Cass now wanted to grab Mexico, Peru, and Cuba as well. This was too much for most Americans, who elected Whig General Zachary Taylor instead.

As conflict grew between the slave and free states, a split developed within Democratic ranks. At their 1860 convention, Southern Democrats, infuriated by abolitionist party members in the North, demanded that the party take a stand for the "divine institution" of slavery. When Northern Democrats balked, delegates from Alabama, Mississippi, Florida, Texas, South Carolina, North Carolina, Louisiana, Georgia, Arkansas, and Delaware walked out.

The Northern Democrats then nominated Stephen A. Douglas as the official party candidate. The Southern Democrats angrily nominated their own candidate, John C. Breckinridge, who actually won 72 Electoral College votes to Douglas's 12. This Democratic split allowed Republican Lincoln to win.

After the Civil War the Democrats benefited from a solid Democratic vote in the South, because of the bitterness of Southern whites against the Republicans for ending slavery and for stationing federal troops down South to protect blacks. But the Democrats rapidly lost ground elsewhere because America entered a phase of great economic expansion, and most voters saw the Republicans as the party best able to achieve the American dream for every citizen.

For 64 years the only president the Democrats were able to elect was Grover Cleveland (twice) until Woodrow Wilson in 1912. And Wilson's election occurred only because of a split in the Republican Party between President William H. Taft and the bolting Bull Moose faction of Theodore Roosevelt.

At the Democratic Convention the corrupt Tammany Hall political organization of New York put forth the nomination of Rep. James Clark of Missouri. Opposition to him was led by William Jennings Bryan, who thundered, "We hereby declare ourselves opposed to the nomination of any candidate for president under obligation to J. Pierpont Morgan . . . or any other member of the privilege-hunting and favor-seeking class!"

A near riot ensued when one furious New York delegate rose to yell, "I offer $25,000 to the man who will kill William Jennings Bryan! Kill him! Hang him!" But only Clark's nomination was killed.

The stormy Democratic Convention took 46 ballots to decide, finally, on a compromise candidate—Governor Woodrow Wilson of New Jersey. His administration produced two important changes in the image of the Democratic Party. The taint of corruption faded because of Wilson's reputation as a thoroughly honest politician. And because of his passionate effort to bring the United States into the League of Nations, the Democrats became identified with international efforts to work for world peace.

The Republicans, endorsing Washington's policy of "no foreign entanglements," attacked the Democrats as the party that pledged peace, then took the country into war. They subsequently pointed out that all our wars from World War I on—World War II, Korea, and Vietnam—had been begun under Democratic administrations.

American disillusionment with World War I and the League of Nations turned the Democrats out of power for the next 12 years. Prosperity during the 1920's gave Republican candidates an easy time of it until the Great Depression suddenly materialized under the administration of Herbert Hoover.

Then frightened Americans turned back to the Democrats for a change in direction. Under Franklin D. Roosevelt, the Democrats once more emerged as the party of the common people. F.D.R.'s "New Deal" promised to provide jobs, unemployment relief, support for a dynamic trade-union movement, aid to small farmers, a moratorium on mortgage foreclosures, Social Security for the aged, and other vital measures to rescue imperiled Americans. They supported him enthusiastically.

The Republicans charged Roosevelt and the Democrats with introducing "communism" into the American system. The Democrats replied that because the nation's economic machinery had broken down, with a threat of revolution developing, the Democrats had saved the capitalist system by reforming it.

The thirteen Roosevelt years in the White House stamped the Democratic Party as indelibly dedicated to government action to solve the economic problems of the nation. The millions who elected Roosevelt four times felt that he had a sympathetic understanding of their difficulties and was determined to use government programs to come to their rescue. Even when some of his programs failed, voters were grateful to him for making the effort.

The Republicans, however, charged that the Democrats had not really been able to solve the unemployment problem until the threat from Nazi Germany had compelled the United States to put its defense industries into high gear.

The Democrats were given high marks by voters for the successful prosecution of World War II. But there was grave doubt after Roosevelt's death in office that the Democrats had another candidate who could fill his shoes. The vice-president who succeeded him, Harry S Truman, was attacked by the Republicans for being "soft on communism" and tolerating an administration riddled with communists. Demagogues like Senator Joseph McCarthy of Wisconsin stirred national hysteria with unfounded and fraudulent charges, accusing the Democrats of "twenty years of treason." Forced on the defensive after the war, the Democrats had lost control of both houses of Congress.

They ran into further trouble when Southerners grew furious over Truman's determination to press for civil rights legislation. In 1948 the Southern Democrats formed a third party called the Dixiecrats, with Governor Strom Thurmond of South Carolina as their presidential candidate. Truman's hopes of staying in the Oval Office were further dampened when he angered former Vice-President Henry Wallace, who felt that Truman had betrayed the Democratic Party's liberal traditions. Wallace formed the Progressive Party to oppose him for the liberal vote.

Running against Republican opponent Governor Thomas E. Dewey of New York, as well as Democratic rivals on the right and left, Truman made a 60,000-mile whistle-stop train tour of the country. Supporters delighted by his blunt campaign oratory cried, "Give 'em hell, Harry!" The underdog in the election, he was given no chance by the opinion polls to win. "The President's influence," observed *The New York Times*, "is weaker than any President's has been in modern history."

Truman later recalled the events of election night:

"At six o'clock I was defeated," he said. "At ten o'clock I was defeated. Twelve o'clock I was defeated. Four o'clock I had won the election. And the next morning . . . in St. Louis, I was handed this paper which said, DEWEY DEFEATS TRUMAN!"

Grinning, he held up the mistaken newspaper for photographers to record the historic journalistic blunder.

But the Democrats swiftly became aware that, despite holding the White House, they had a permanent, serious problem in Congress with the conservative Southern wing of their party. Those "Boll Weevil" Democrats did not hesitate to make deals with Republicans against the programs of liberal Northern Democrats. This split persisted even into

Although the split between Democrats resulted in Stephen A. Douglas receiving 12 electoral votes to John Breckinridge's 72, Douglas is the more famous man because of the Lincoln–Douglas debates.

William Jennings Bryan, unsuccessful candidate for president in 1896, 1900, and 1908, in the heat of a vigorous speech. PHOTO COPYRIGHT 1908.

Incumbent President Harry Truman was considered a certain loser in the 1948 election, as evidenced by the famous banner headline here, mistakenly announcing his defeat.

the Reagan administration thirty years later, when they would often vote against their own party for Republican bills.

In 1952 an Eisenhower landslide swept the Democrats out of the White House. They were not able to return until 1960, when the charisma of John F. Kennedy prevailed. A new wave of idealism swept the Democratic Party. Kennedy—young, handsome, articulate, vigorous—struck sparks among his fellow Democrats by crying, "Ask not what your country can do for you; ask what you can do for your country!" Youth, in particular, was swept up in an idealistic fervor. The Kennedy administration was revered as the "new Camelot."

But the new President sent confusing signals to his starry-eyed followers, most of whom were dedicated to keeping the nation at peace. He mounted the Bay of Pigs invasion of Castro's Cuba, which proved a disastrous failure. When Cuba reacted by allowing the Soviet Union to base missiles on its soil, Kennedy brought the world to brink of nuclear war by blockading Soviet ships headed for Havana. War was averted only by a last-minute Soviet agreement to remove the missiles, in exchange for a U.S. pledge not to invade Cuba.

Finally, Kennedy intervened in the Vietnam civil war by sending American advisers and aid to South Vietnam.

Democratic intensification of the Cold War did not end with Kennedy's assassination in November, 1963. His successor, Lyndon B. Johnson, escalated American intervention in Vietnam to the extent of committing half a million U.S. troops to fight in that unhappy land. Disclosures of atrocities they committed against Vietnam civilians shocked and revolted the country. American college students, and gradually many Americans of all ages, became so disillusioned with the Democrats that the country was swept by massive anti-war demonstrations.

At the same time, President Johnson's domestic policies favored the poor and minorities, in the tradition of his political idol, Franklin D. Roosevelt. He assured Americans that the nation could afford both guns and butter, but in actuality he ran up an enormous national debt leading to inflation. More and more his "Great Society" program was neglected as he persisted in trying to win the Vietnam War.

Disillusionment with the Johnson administration split the Democratic Party, making it clear he could not be reelected. Senator George McGovern told *The New York Times* reporter Tom Wicker, "I've made up my mind.... I'm going to run for president and the coalition I'm going to put together is going to be built around the poor and the minorities and the young people and the anti-war movement."

The McGovern forces shook up the structure of the Democratic Party by forcing the selection of delegates to be more representative. Those who assembled for the 1972 Democratic Convention were far younger and more liberal, with a larger representation of women, than at any previous convention.

Awarded the presidential nomination, McGovern called it "all the more precious in that it is the gift of the most open political process in our national history."

But the party's professional politicians, disgruntled by the "bunch of amateurs" who had taken over, largely abstained from the campaign. McGovern lost every state in the election except Massachusetts. "We opened the doors and windows to the Democratic Party," he joked wryly afterward, "and everybody walked out." With the party in disarray and in the doldrums, Democratic chances for a comeback looked bleak.

The Watergate scandal of the Nixon administration renewed their hopes for 1976. In the Democratic scramble for the nomination, Jimmy Carter bypassed party leaders and made himself the front-runner by campaigning hard in the primaries. Winning over Republican President Gerald Ford, Carter tried to give the new Democratic administration a "common man" flavor by walking instead of riding to his inauguration and by carrying his own clothes on hangers off the presidential plane.

But Carter seemed indecisive and lacking in leadership qualities to many Americans, especially in his handling of the Iranian hostage crisis. So he became a one-term President, and once more the Democrats fell out of power.

Democratic leaders decided that the McGovern reforms had weakened the party too much. Changes were subsequently made in the rules so that almost 600 congressmen, senators, governors, and state party chairmen were granted delegate status.

The Democratic Party has always been the one that kept an ear open to what third parties were saying, in order to co-opt policies that seemed to have great appeal for special voting blocs in American society. Franklin D. Roosevelt's New Deal program was made up in part from ideas advocated by American socialists and progressives. The Democrats can be expected to continue this tradition, whenever there is widespread public dissatisfaction and some third party seems to have a popular answer to the problem.

The party's newest rules, adopted during the Reagan administration, attempted to shorten the campaign season by creating a thirteen-week period during which states could hold primaries or caucuses, with Iowa and New Hampshire compelled to delay theirs to conform. This change was intended to make campaigning less costly and avoid wearying voters. But dark-horse candidates felt this would unfairly favor better-known Democrats, not giving them sufficient time to win national recognition and campaign funding.

Reagan's resounding victory in 1980 made it seem as though the whole country had turned Republican. But the fact was that there were still far more registered Democrats than Republicans. That is why, although voters may elect a popular Republican to the White House, they invariably vote a heavy percentage of Democrats into the House of Representatives. They count on a Democratic House to protect their economic benefits.

The Democrats also enjoy the important support of most black voters, who have become increasingly active politically. The almost 100 percent black voter turnout in Chicago in 1983 for Mayor Harold Washington demonstrated the power of a united black vote. To keep the loyalty of blacks, Democrats generally include planks in their platform that respond to black demands, and they give blacks important roles within the party. In 1982 blacks were shown to hold 5,000 elected offices at the local level, usually through Democratic campaigns.

On the other hand, the white South is no longer solidly Democratic. Many Southerners, antagonized by the Democrats' civil rights policies, have been permanently wooed away by the Republican Party. Also, the migration of many middle-class, conservative Northerners to the South has led to a further decline in the Southern Democratic vote.

The Democrats today suffer somewhat in public opinion from the

Republicans' persistent campaign to depict them as the spendthrift "party of bureaucracy." This was the thrust of Ronald Reagan's successful 1980 campaign for the presidency to "get government off the backs of the people."

Democrats today have a wide-open door for young people they hope to involve in their politics. Their Teen Dem program for teenagers operates in a number of states, and they seek to encourage the formation of more such clubs. The party offers an organizational manual that tells how to set one up.

"These young people, working after school hours, were extremely valuable to our Democratic organization," declared former Indiana Senator Birch Bayh, "and I believe will become valuable workers for the senior party in later years."

The Young Democratic Club of America was formed in 1932 to give young people a significant role in the party's councils. President Franklin D. Roosevelt told them at the time, "America will have to be led in the days to come by the youth of today. . . . You will find that your fight against selfishness and injustice, against oppression, and above all, against war, will take you into a man-sized struggle."

Those reasons still appeal to young people today who view the Democratic Party as the instrument for achieving those objectives, and who are willing to get involved.

Further information can be obtained from the Democratic National Committee, 1625 Massachusetts Avenue N.W., Washington, D.C. 20036.

8

WHAT THE REPUBLICANS
ARE ALL ABOUT

Will Rogers, the famous cowboy-comedian of the 1920's, was once asked what made an American citizen become a Republican. "Wa-al," he replied, chewing gum and twirling his lariat, "when a Democrat scrapes together ten bucks, that's when he becomes a Republican."

This wry joke reflected the commonly held concept that Democrats were the party of the poor, while Republicans represented the well-to-do classes. It also suggested that as soon as many Americans at the bottom of the economic ladder saw an improvement in their prospects, they became ambitious to join the ranks of the prosperous Republicans. The Republican vote usually soared in times of prosperity.

According to the Teen Age Republicans (TAR), the Republican Party today stands for six major principles:

1. Decentralization of power and building up local units of government.

2. Protection of private enterprise, freed of all regulations except those absolutely necessary to safeguard the public interest.

3. Curbing inflation.

4. Protection of Constitutional liberties.

5. Rejection of class struggle.

6. Balance of power among the branches of government.

The senior Republican Party adds to those goals:

7. A sound money policy.

8. Opposition to excessive taxation and government waste.

9. Maintaining a strong military.

10. Getting people off welfare rolls by assisting them to become productive and self-supporting.

11. Developing individual responsibility and initiative among Americans.

The Democrats accuse the Republican Party of traditionally siding with business against union labor; favoring the elimination of social welfare programs; seeking the suppression of liberal and left-wing ideas; favoring big business over small business; opposing conservation and pressing for private exploitation of America's resources; giving aid to right-wing military dictatorships while seeking to overthrow left-wing governments; favoring big military expenditures and an aggressive foreign policy, while opposing anti-nuclear and peace movements.

The Republican Party, however, has its liberals as well as right-wingers, and there is often sharp disagreement between them. At the 1964 Republican Convention in San Francisco, liberal Republicans led by New York's Governor Nelson Rockefeller tried to add an anti-extremist plank to the party platform.

The presidential nominee, Arizona Senator Barry Goldwater, objected, declaring, "I would remind you that extremism in the defense of liberty is no vice." The plank was defeated.

Next year, after Goldwater's defeat, liberal Republican Senator Charles Percy of Illinois called upon right-wing extremists to get out of Republican ranks and form their own political party. "The fanatical pseudo-patriotism of these men is misdirected," he charged.

George E. Reedy, former press secretary and special assistant to President Lyndon Johnson, observed, "The Democratic Party has continuing trouble with left-wing crackpots, and the Republican Party has continuing trouble with right-wing crackpots."

Denying that conservatives are reactionary extremists, the Republican Party states, "The conservative ideals of the Republican Party represent true progress. . . . The Republican Party believes that government is the servant and not the master of the people. . . . The constantly growing federal power as espoused by the Democrat Party can come only at the expense of the individual."

The majority of Republicans are Protestants, with above-average educations, above-average incomes, and high-status occupations, living outside the South. Generally they tend to identify the national interest with the interest of the higher socioeconomic classes. Unlike the Democrats, they believe that the federal government should cut business taxes to create jobs by stimulating prosperity, rather than by helping the jobless directly.

As explained by President Ronald Reagan, the corporations would invest tax savings in new plants and equipment, which in turn would put more people to work. The Democratic rebuttal is that this "trickle-down" theory is misleading, because the corporations use their tax savings only to buy up other companies and fatten their profits.

The Republican Party came into being in 1855 because abolitionist lawyer Alvan E. Boray was disillusioned by the failure of both the Whig and Democratic Parties to stop the spread of slavery. He appealed to his old friend Horace Greeley, editor-publisher of the influential New York *Tribune*, to support a new third party he and other abolitionists were forming.

Greeley agreed, telling Bovay, "Call your party Republican. No prefix, no suffix—just plain Republican!"

The new party attracted various splinter groups—abolitionists, Free Soilers, prohibitionists, Know-Nothings (afterward the American Party), dissident Whigs like Lincoln, and anti-slavery Democrats like William Cullen Bryant, the leading Democratic editor in New York.

Greeley joined in organizing the first Republican National Convention in Philadelphia on June 17, 1856. To oppose the Whig nominee, former President Millard Fillmore, and Democratic nominee James Buchanan, the Republicans nominated Colonel John C. Frémont of California. He was the famous "Pathfinder" whose expeditions had helped open the West.

"Enthusiasm tremendous!" Greeley wired his paper. As he viewed the three-cornered election, the chief issue was whether the West would be "blessed with Freedom or cursed with Slavery." Moreover, who better than the Pathfinder could be relied upon to develop the West with rails, roads, and waterways?

Greeley's arguments swelled the ranks of the new Republican Party. But the wealthy conservative interests behind both Buchanan and Fillmore spent ten times as much on each candidate's campaign as the Republicans could raise for Frémont. The Republicans were portrayed as "wild-eyed abolitionists" whose victory would provoke a Southern rebellion.

Buchanan won with 1,838,000 votes, but Frémont received 1,335,000 votes, an impressive showing for a new third party. The Whigs, whose nominee was also supported by the American Party, received only a humiliating 874,000 votes, ending their life as a political party. From this time forward the Democrats and Republicans were America's two major parties.

The Republicans' opportunity came in 1860, when Buchanan's demand that Kansas be admitted to the Union as a slave state tore the Democratic Party in half. The Republicans chose as their presidential nominee Abraham Lincoln, whom Greeley had lifted to national prominence by publicizing his debates with Senator Stephen A. Douglas.

When Lincoln defeated the two feuding Democratic candidates running against him, it was Greeley who rode with him on the presidential train to the first Republican inauguration. But Greeley's support gradually ebbed as he grew convinced that Lincoln was turning a deaf ear to the public outcry against the bloody Civil War, refusing to talk peace with the South. In 1864 Greeley's opposition split the Republican Party into two wings. The Radicals nominated Frémont, while the National Union Party combined with War Democrats to renominate Lincoln in support of the war effort.

Lincoln's aides worked hard to persuade the influential Greeley to change his mind, finally succeeding two months before election day. Greeley's defection from the Radicals took Frémont out of the race. The Republicans then reunited behind Lincoln, reelecting him easily.

The Republican Party dominated national politics throughout the last half of the nineteenth century and the first part of the twentieth. Although the party alienated Southern white votes because of the

Republicans' enforcement of black voting rights in the South, they more than made up for this loss by turning out a heavy Northern vote for their candidates. They did this by stirring memories of Civil War passions with the slogan: "Vote As You Shot!"

One of the more colorful Republican figures at the close of the nineteenth century was William McKinley's campaign manager, Mark Hanna. In 1896 he plastered the country with billboards advertising McKinley's candidacy, leading Theodore Roosevelt to complain, "Hanna was selling McKinley like a patent medicine." Hanna directed big companies to threaten their employees with closing their plants if McKinley wasn't elected.

Hanna spent $3,500,000 on McKinley's campaign, an unprecedented sum raised by levies on businessmen and corporations.

As President, McKinley presided over the only American war begun under a Republican administration. His Secretary of State, John Hay, called the Spanish-American War "a splendid little war." Spain was forced to cede to the American victors the Philippines, Puerto Rico, and Guam and to yield Cuba to the American sphere of influence.

In the election campaign of 1900, William Jennings Bryan led the Democrats in opposing what they termed American imperialism. McKinley and his vice-presidential candidate, Theodore Roosevelt, defended the Spanish-American War and its territorial acquisitions. The Republicans won.

Roosevelt became President the following year when McKinley was assassinated. He committed the Republican Party to an expansionist foreign policy by seeking naval supremacy, making the United States the dominant power in the Pacific and in Central and South America. To give our navy quick passage between the Atlantic and Pacific, he decided to build a canal through a narrow pinch of Colombia's land.

He conspired with a military junta in Colombia, which revolted and seized the land he wanted. Roosevelt then recognized them as the "Republic of Panama," and two hours later he had the grant to build the Panama Canal. When a hot quarrel over his grab broke out in Congress, Roosevelt said, "I took the Canal Zone, and let Congress debate, and while the debate goes on, the Canal does also."

A colorful, dynamic president, he was popular with the people in the

New York Tribune *editor Horace Greeley (seated) was instrumental in the formation of the Republican party in 1855. He, in fact, gave the party its name.* PHOTO BY BOGARDUS.

The number of votes Republican John C. Frémont received in the 1856 election heralded the downfall of the Whig Party. Since 1856, the Democrats and the Republicans have been America's two major parties. LITHOGRAPH BY CURRIER AND IVES.

street, but surprisingly less so with corporation executives. They saw him as a reformer out to restrict their operations with such bills as the Pure Food and Drug Act and the Hepburn Act controlling rates the railroads could charge. But the muckrakers—reform-minded journalists of that day—charged Roosevelt with only faking a crusade against big-business abuses to fool the public.

Big business, fearing that a Democratic administration would pay more attention to the muckrakers, supported Roosevelt for a term of his own in 1904.

Roosevelt helped elect his friend William Howard Taft as his successor in 1908. But the two men fell out when Taft refused to let Roosevelt be the power behind the throne.

At the Republican Convention in 1912, Roosevelt sought to prevent Taft's renomination, attacking him as a "hopeless" reactionary. When the Republicans chose Taft anyhow, Roosevelt bolted the party angrily. "The fight is on," he snapped, "and I am fit as a bull moose!" He arranged for his own nomination by a third party, the Progressives, which became known as the Bull Moose Party.

Roosevelt's dynamic campaigning beat Taft by almost 632,000 votes. But the split Republican vote gave the election to the Democratic candidate, Woodrow Wilson, who subsequently led the nation into World War I. Had there been no third party to thwart Taft's reelection, the course of world history might have been changed, since Taft deplored war, favoring arbitration to solve international disagreements.

The Republicans were restored to power in 1922 through Senator Warren Harding, who appealed to an electorate weary of World War I and foreign entanglements by promising a "return to normalcy." At that point the Republican Party committed itself to an isolationist policy—staying apart from Europe's incessant quarrels.

Harding had one solid achievement during his administration—a five-power naval-disarmament conference in Washington. But his administration fell into disrepute when he surrounded himself with trusted politicians who proved corrupt, plundering the nation's naval oil reserves for personal profit.

The scandal, however, did not end Republican control of the White House. When Harding died in office, he was succeeded by Vice-

President Calvin Coolidge, a taciturn New Englander who rarely said one word more than necessary. In 1924 Coolidge was elected for a term of his own on a platform of "Coolidge prosperity." Business, Coolidge insisted, was "America's chief business."

As president he maintained high tariffs to protect American industries, curbed government regulation of business, eliminated and slashed taxes on corporations and wealthy individuals, and reduced both the national debt and the national budget. Coolidge set a precedent for Republicans who followed him to exercise federal powers as little as possible, allowing the free-enterprise market to regulate itself.

As long as business remained prosperous and jobs were plentiful, Americans kept voting the Republicans back into office. In 1928 Herbert Hoover succeeded Coolidge as President. Unfortunately for him, overheated stock speculation brought on a market crash on "Black Thursday," October 24, 1929, followed by the worst economic depression in American history. Over 15 million Americans found themselves without jobs.

Hoover's dogged belief in "rugged individualism," based on his own career, held that courageous and determined Americans could shape their own fortunes. This outlook did not go down well with desperate Americans thrown out of work.

To make matters worse for the Republicans, Hoover committed a grievous error in judgment. In 1932 over 20,000 jobless veterans and their families joined a Bonus Army march to Washington to demand prompt payment of war bonuses promised them. Hoover ordered out the Army with tanks to chase them out of the capital. Pictures of American troops using bayonets and tear gas against the nation's veterans horrified the public, dooming Republican chances in 1932.

In a desperate attempt to hold onto the White House, Hoover appealed, "This thirty years of incomparable improvement in the scale of living . . . did not arise without right principles animating the American system which produced them. Shall that system be discarded because vote-seeking men appeal to distress and say that the machinery is all wrong and that it must be abandoned or tampered with?"

But American voters, disillusioned with the Hoover administration, swept it out of power by an overwhelming vote. The Democrats were then able to hold power for the next twenty years, during which the thrust of American policy was turned completely away from the Republican emphasis on uncontrolled private enterprise to the Democratic emphasis on government intervention in the American system.

During that period most Republicans favored isolationism, staying clear of the growing war clouds in Europe. The Democrats urged the need to render aid to European democracies facing the threat of Nazi Germany and Fascist Italy. Only after the Japanese attack on Pearl Harbor in 1941 did the Republicans reluctantly support President Franklin Roosevelt's entry into World War II.

When Roosevelt died and was succeeded by Vice-President Harry S Truman, voters became disaffected by Washington scandals and incompetence exposed by reporters. The Republicans capitalized on public anger by their Congressional campaign slogan in 1946: "Had Enough?" Voters gave them massive gains in both houses of Congress.

The Republicans mounted Congressional investigations that sought to picture Truman's administration as riddled with communist spies and sympathizers. Meanwhile Republican Party leaders split on the choice of a presidential candidate for 1952. Isolationists wanted Senator Robert A. Taft of Ohio, while the party's internationalists backed New York Governor Thomas Dewey.

In an effort to unify the two factions, party leaders persuaded General Dwight D. Eisenhower to run instead. He was the perfect compromise because he spoke in generalities that offended neither side. He was also one of the most popular men in American life, both with ex-G.I.s and the general public. Even Democrats wore "I Like Ike" campaign buttons.

Elected, Eisenhower worked tirelessly to reduce tensions between the United States and the Soviet Union. His rigid secretary of state, John Foster Dulles, took a hard line instead. The two reflected the conflicting views within the Republican Party. In the end Eisenhower took over the direction of foreign policy himself, to keep hotheads from pressing the United States into a war situation.

The Korean War, which had begun under Truman, was stalemated when Eisenhower took office. In just a few months he ended it with an armistice—a peace without victory, but a peace. The Democrats complained that if they had done the same thing, they would have been accused of "appeasing communism." But no one dreamed of bringing such an accusation against a distinguished Republican war hero.

Eisenhower also had the courage to propose universal disarmament, declaring, "Every gun that is made, every warship launched, every rocket fired signifies . . . a theft from those who hunger and are not fed, those who are cold and not clothed. . . . We pay for a single destroyer with new homes that could have housed more than eight thousand people."

He also warned the American people against letting the military-industrial complex acquire unnecessary influence, because this would lead to a shocking waste of the nation's resources and a growth of militarism. "We must never let the weight of this combination," he warned, "endanger our liberties or democratic processes."

Although Eisenhower was easily reelected in 1956, his personal popularity did not carry over to his "coattails"—other Republican candidates on the ticket. Both houses of Congress fell under the control of the Democrats.

The extremist wing of the Republican Party, led by Senator Joseph McCarthy, persisted in trying to portray the Democratic Party as "riddled with communism." McCarthy used unscrupulous methods to smear and damage many innocent people. He was angrily opposed by Eisenhower, especially after McCarthy began to attack U.S. Army generals. When the Senate finally destroyed McCarthy's power by a vote condemning his conduct, Eisenhower warmly congratulated the Senators.

After Eisenhower, the Republicans fell out of power for another eight years. In 1968 Richard M. Nixon was elected president as a result of the split in the Democratic Party over the Vietnam War. Instead of ending it as he had promised, Nixon widened the war for another four years. Angry protest demonstrations kept the country in an uproar. Not until Nixon's second term was a peace finally signed, on virtually the same terms Nixon could have had four years earlier.

On the other hand, Nixon was given high marks for opening a new door to the People's Republic of China. His "journey for peace" to Beijing in 1972 normalized relations with that country, ending 24 years of mu-

Theodore Roosevelt at the Panama
Canal: "I took the Canal Zone, and
let Congress debate, and while the
debate goes on, the Canal does
also." PEN AND INK DRAWING BY CLIFFORD
K. BERRYMAN.

October, 1920: Senator Warren
Harding arriving in Washington.
Later, as president, he surrounded
himself with reputable politicians
who proved corrupt. PHOTO COPYRIGHT
1920 BY HARRIS & EWING.

Republican Dwight D. Eisenhower,
president from 1952 until 1960, was
so popular that even Democrats
wore his campaign buttons.

tual hostility. Only a Republican president with Nixon's history of rigid anti-communism could have made that move without provoking angry cries of "appeasing communism." This triumph of international diplomacy helped reelect him in 1972.

Republicans became dismayed, however, when the *Washington Post* exposed the notorious Watergate scandal. The Nixon administration was revealed as using dirty tricks and illegal campaign tactics against the Democrats, then committing crimes to cover up their felonies. Nixon sought to spike congressional and court investigations by insisting that "national security" prevented him from supplying subpoenaed evidence.

He also tried to keep aides from being forced to testify on grounds that their conversations with the president were protected by "presidential privilege." But the Watergate scandal grew so great that outraged Republicans as well as Democrats were ready to impeach him. To avoid that disgrace, Nixon resigned and Vice-President Gerald Ford took his place. Many of Nixon's top aides were convicted and jailed.

To soothe shaken Americans, Ford promised a clean and open administration. His conduct in the White House did much to restore public confidence in the government.

When Ford failed to win a term of his own, the Republicans did not return to power until 1980, with the election of Ronald Reagan. Charging that "big government" spending was the cause of inflation, Reagan moved swiftly to reduce taxes and the federal budget, except for military spending. The new thrust of Republican policy sought to dismantle as much federal apparatus as possible, turning its functions over to state and local governments for funding and control.

The Reagan administration produced a dramatic drop in the inflation rate but also a severe business recession that caused widespread unemployment. Reagan blamed that on preceding Democratic administrations. During his first two years in office he proved skillful at manipulating Congress, getting most of the legislation he wanted out of a Republican-controlled Senate and a Democratic House, by winning the votes of the conservative "Boll Weevil" Southerners.

Reagan was also skillful in handling the "New Right," a coalition of ultra-conservative groups that had helped elect him. He needed to keep their support, while at the same time not offending Republican liberals and moderates and independent voters, who viewed the New Right as an extremist pressure group.

Reagan's solution was to appear before New Right convocations to support with resounding oratory their goals of voluntary school prayers, a ban on abortion, a ban on busing for integration, discrimination against homosexuals, opposition to the Equal Rights Amendment, and censorship of TV, films, and magazines that offended their values. Their cheers and applause obscured the fact that Reagan was careful not to try to press such legislation through Congress.

Reagan's policies abroad showed a return to the expansionist military philosophy of Theodore Roosevelt. He gave military aid to right-wing governments like El Salvador, and also to right-wing guerrillas fighting to overthrow the leftist government of Nicaragua, dubbing them "freedom fighters."

Controversy arose when a peace-keeping force of U.S. Marines he sent to strife-torn Lebanon in 1983 was attacked by terrorists, who killed 237. More controversy occurred when he sent Marines to invade the Caribbean island of Grenada to overthrow the Cuban-influenced Communist government there as a threat to U.S. security, claiming it was necessary to rescue American medical students. The U.N. condemned the invasion, but the majority of Americans supported it.

The Republican Party has never lacked for Democratic critics. In 1915 Woodrow Wilson said, "The trouble with the Republican Party is that it has not had a new idea for 30 years. I am not speaking as a politician; I am speaking as an historian."

And in 1955 Lyndon B. Johnson avowed, "The Democratic Party at its worst is better for the country than the Republican Party at its best."

Political cynic Arthur Pearl, professor of education at the University of California, Santa Cruz, observed wryly, "If a man doesn't know anything about a job before he's elected to it, he's probably a Democrat. If he doesn't know anything after holding a job for four years, he's a Republican."

If the Democratic Party can be said to occupy the liberal-to-center side of the political spectrum, the Republicans in general can be found in the center-to-conservative side. But both parties try to give the appearance of being as close to the center as possible, where most votes are usually found.

As the Republicans see themselves today, they are the party of fiscal sanity; of defenders of the people against the excesses of big government; of encouragement for the exponents of free enterprise to create prosperity; of making America so militarily strong that no nation will dare attack us.

Like the Democrats, the Republicans welcome teenagers to join their ranks. "I know nothing more encouraging for the future of our party," Ronald Reagan declared, "than Teen Age Republicans." Over 80,000 TARS are active in almost 2,000 TAR clubs around the country.

Teens interested in joining may write to National TAR Headquarters, 1010 Vermont Avenue N.W., Washington, D.C. 20005, to learn where their nearest local unit is located. TAR will also provide a manual for any teenager interested in organizing a chapter in his or her own district.

9

WHAT THIRD PARTIES
ARE ALL ABOUT

New Yorkers were upset when scandal after scandal erupted in their city hall under a Democratic mayor in 1933. Angered Republican Congressman Fiorello H. La Guardia, known as "the Little Flower," vowed to clean up his beloved city by returning home to run for mayor. But Republican Party leaders in New York refused to nominate him. La Guardia was too liberal for their taste. So he decided to run on a new third-party ticket. His Fusion Party appealed to New Yorkers to support him and restore the city to good government.

"Isn't it *grand?*" La Guardia grinned to reporters. "Not a single county leader of either political party is endorsing me. Well, as Al Smith used to say, 'I could run on a laundry ticket and beat those political bums!'"

The third-party candidate was as good as his word. Winning the election easily, he booted corrupt officials out of the city government and delighted New Yorkers by his refreshing honesty and eccentricity, which included a lisping reading of comic strips on the radio to the city's kids during a newspaper strike. He was reelected in 1937 and 1941.

When elections are discussed, usually the only parties mentioned are the Republicans and the Democrats. But there are many more seeking to challenge both at the polls. The nation's principal third parties are the American Independent Party, American Party of the United States, Communist Party U.S.A., Conservative Party of the State of New York, Liberal Party of New York State, Libertarian National Committee, National States' Rights Party, Socialist Party, Socialist Labor Party, and Socialist Workers Party.

All have in common a distrust of the two major parties, between which they profess to see no real difference. Many third parties are oriented around a basic issue, such as labor, socialism, communism, states' rights, law and order, etc.

Professional politicians disdain the efforts of third parties to win elections. Nevertheless they sometimes influence the outcome of tight races, denying the margin of votes needed for victory to a major-party candidate. And from time to time they do manage to elect their own candidates both to Congress and to state legislatures, as well as to city halls.

Today's two major parties were originally third parties themselves. By 1803 both the Federalist and Anti-Federalist Parties were dominated by wealthy men. Jefferson broke away from the Anti-Federalists to challenge both with a new third party that spoke for the people—the Democratic-Republican Party. And in 1856 the Republican Party emerged to challenge both the Democrats and the Whigs.

The earliest party to advocate class struggle in America appeared in 1828, following the failure of a Mechanics Union strike. This was the Workingman's Labor Party of Philadelphia, which campaigned for a ten-hour workday. The following year they held a convention in New York, where they denounced "hereditary transmission of wealth on the one hand and poverty on the other" as twin evils. Calling for an end to all privileges and monopolies, they castigated bankers as "the greatest knaves, imposters . . . of the age." They demanded identical education for children of the poor and the rich, up to and through college—"as in a real republic, it should be."

In a campaign song, the "Workies" called upon all American workers to desert the major parties:

Mechanics, cartmen, laborers
Must form a close connection,
And show the rich Aristocrats,
Their powers at this election.

At first, professional politicians scoffed at the Workingman's Party as a bad joke. But when its candidate for mayor of New York polled 30 percent of the vote, it was taken seriously. The United States Bank, through its mouthpiece, the New York *Courier and Enquirer*, assailed party members as "immoral infidels whose doctrines threaten to topple the very foundations of private property and the American Republic."

The New York state legislature took a more adroit tack. By introducing a few "reform" bills that paid lip service to some of the party's demands, but actually changed little, legislative leaders flattered the party's firebrands into easing their crusade. By 1831 the movement was becalmed, with no more wind in its sails.

The drive of the Workingman's Party for universal education picked up new steam, however, with the emergence in 1831 of another third party, the New England Association of Farmers, Mechanics, and Other Workmen. In addition to agitating for the ten-hour workday, this party pressed hard for free public schools.

The great acceleration of immigration during the 1840's, with many immigrants coming from Catholic countries, provoked a strong anti-immigrant, anti-Catholic movement similar to the kind of hostility we see today directed toward recent immigrants from Mexico, Cuba, Puerto Rico, Vietnam, Haiti, and El Salvador.

Small extremist groups like the Order of the Star-Spangled Banner, the Order of United Americans, the American Protestant Society, and the American and Foreign Christian Union amalgamated into one new party called the Native American Party, derisively branded the Know-Nothings by Horace Greeley.

Their intolerance poisoned the minds of millions of Americans with anti-Catholic suspicion. Every Catholic cardinal, they charged, was really a spy and inquisitor for the pope, sent to America "for the sole purpose of opposing, persecuting, and fighting against the Protestant . . . community."

Know-Nothing candidates showed impressive strength at the polls, almost capturing New York State, winning in Massachusetts, and electing governors in nine other states. In Congress, 8 out of 62 senators and 104 out of 234 representatives, were avowed Know-Nothings. Catholics and immigrants grew dismayed and frightened in the land that had promised religious liberty, justice, and equality for all.

When the Know-Nothings obtained control, declared Abraham Lincoln angrily, the Declaration of Independence would be amended to read, "'All men are created equal except Negroes, foreigners, and Catholics.'"

The Know-Nothings fielded pro-slavery ex-President Millard Fillmore as their presidential candidate in 1856. Their campaign urged factory workers to vote for Fillmore as a vote against "cheap-working foreigners." When he finished a poor third behind the two major-party candidates, the Know-Nothings went into a rapid decline.

The earliest abolitionist party was the Liberty Party, which met at New York in 1843 to nominate James G. Birney for president. In the presidential elections the following year, the race was so close between Democrat James Polk and Whig Henry Clay that if Birney's 62,300 votes had gone to Clay instead, he would have become president instead of Polk, and the Mexican War might never have taken place.

Another early third party was the Barnburners. Opposed to the extension of slavery, they joined with the Liberty Party in 1848 to support a new Free Soil Party, which had as its slogan, "Free soil, free speech, free labor, and free men."

Leading abolitionist William Lloyd Garrison called the Free Soilers "unmistakable proof of the progress we have made, under God, in changing public sentiment." Their candidate in 1848 was former Democratic President Martin Van Buren. Had their vote gone instead to Democratic candidate Lewis Cass, he would have become president instead of Whig Zachary Taylor.

Following the Civil War, many Americans felt that the government was aiding the corporations and special interests but neglecting farmers, workers, and the poor. A new Greenback Party formed in 1875 to demand the issuance of greenbacks—paper money with no gold or silver backing. An inflated currency would cause prices to rise, giving farmers more for their crops and letting them pay off their bank loans in cheap money worth less than the hard currency they had borrowed. The Greenbackers also joined the Labor Party in demanding a shorter workday and other social reforms.

When they ran candidates for Congress in 1878, they polled a million votes and elected 15 representatives. But their appeal gradually diminished, and they felt compelled to merge with a newly formed National Anti-Monopoly Party.

This party developed when big-business monopolies began to gouge the public in the late nineteenth century by charging exorbitant rates for food, clothes, homes, furnishings, transportation, light, fuel, matches, whiskey, and bank loans.

The Democrats were quick to steal the new third party's thunder. In 1884 their presidential nominee, Grover Cleveland, began denouncing the big corporations as "the people's masters." Congress was pressured into passing the Sherman Anti-Trust Act outlawing monopolies.

The Anti-Monopoly Party joined other splinter parties like the farm-oriented Grangers to form a new People's Party. These Populists, as they were called, demanded cheap money through free coinage of silver on an equal par with gold; government loans to farmers; a graduated income tax (the rich went untaxed); government ownership and operation of the railroads, telephones, and telegraph; stripping railroads, banks, and big corporations of their huge Western land holdings; an eight-hour workday; adoption of the secret Australian ballot to end vote fraud; and curbing immigration to end the supply of scab labor used to break strikes.

Populist Mary Ellen Lease, known as "the Kansas Pythoness," traveled around the plains urging farmers to "raise less corn and more hell." She told them, "Wall Street owns the country. It is no longer a government of the people, by the people, for the people, but a government of Wall Street, by Wall Street, and for Wall Street. Our laws are the output of a system that clothes rascals in robes and honesty in rags!"

"Socialism!" roared the Eastern press. But the elections of 1890 swept Populists into power in a dozen Southern and Western states and sent 13

In 1904 the Socialist Party was a major third party, with Eugene Debs as its major candidate. LITHOGRAPH, 1904.

Millard Fillmore, pictured here as a candidate for vice-president, was in 1856 the Know-Nothing Party's candidate for president. His loss heralded the party's decline. LITHOGRAPH BY N. CURRIER, COPYRIGHT 1848.

of their candidates to Congress. Within the next generation, as Populists proved the popularity of their demands at the polls, both major parties quickly adopted some of their planks.

In Kansas, Populist Governor L. D. Lewelling spelled out the party's insistence that Washington must protect farmers and workers: "The government must make it possible for the citizen to live by his own labor. ... The people are greater than the law or the statutes, and when a nation sets its heart on doing a great or good thing, it can find a legal way."

The Populists won almost a million and a half votes in the mid-term elections of 1894. In 1896 when the Democrats pledged to introduce silver coinage, making William Jennings Bryan their presidential candidate, the Populists made him their candidate, too. But Bryan still lost narrowly to the Republican candidate of big business, McKinley. After a carbon copy of the election in 1900, a weakened People's Party dropped from the national scene.

One of the oldest third parties in the country was the Prohibition Party, organized in 1869 after over 70 years of vigorous anti-liquor agitation. Although its major aim was to outlaw the manufacture and sale of intoxicating liquors, it also advocated many economic and social reforms that later found their way into major-party platforms.

The Prohibitionists made little headway against the powerful political influence of the brewers for half a century, but they refused to be discouraged. Their action wing, called the Anti-Saloon League of America, was led by a one-woman cyclone named Carrie Nation. She would enter saloons carrying a hatchet and announce, "Men, I have come to save you from a drunkard's fate!" *Wham! Crash!* The bar mirror was shattered, and every glass and bottle on the back bar went next.

Once, when she had smashed a saloon's mirror, a detective rushed in and told her, "Madam, you're under arrest for defacing property!"

"Defacing, nothing!" Carrie shouted. "I am *destroying!*"

Carrie Nation and the zealous Prohibitionists who came after her finally persuaded Congress to pass the Volstead Act of 1919 and subsequently to adopt the Eighteenth Amendment that made Prohibition part of the Constitution. Fourteen years later, however, gangster wars over bootlegging so outraged the public that Prohibition was repealed as a failed experiment.

A new version of the Workingman's Party was formed in 1874, subsequently renaming itself the Socialist Labor Party. It was the first openly socialist party to operate on a national scale. Led by Daniel De Leon, its aim was to overthrow capitalism through a general strike by labor unions.

Another labor party called the Single Tax Party formed in New York in 1886 behind Henry George, who demanded a tax on wealthy landowners based on the increase in the value of their land since its purchase, because they had done nothing to earn or deserve this gain, while farmers and laborers who paid rent for its use grew poorer.

New York labor unions ran George as a reform candidate for mayor in 1886. He was given a good chance of winning against the corrupt Tammany Hall Democratic machine until a bomb exploded in Chicago's Haymarket Square. Blamed on labor radicals, the incident soured public feeling toward labor candidates. George was narrowly defeated, but he still polled more votes than the Republican candidate, Theodore Roosevelt.

In 1894 when oppressed Pullman railroad workers went out on strike, America's railroad tycoons acted quickly to crush the new American Railway Union (ARU) led by Eugene Debs. Federal troops were called out. The power of the press, police, and courts were used to destroy the ARU. Twenty strikers were killed in the ensuing violence, and Debs went to jail for six months. Millions of embittered workers followed him into the Socialist Party of America.

"The issue is socialism versus capitalism," Debs cried. "I am for socialism because I am for humanity!" Running for president, he won 88,000 votes in 1900, almost 900,000 by 1912.

The Socialist Party of America demanded a social-security program; improved labor conditions; housing and welfare legislation; increased educational opportunities; votes for women; and federal control over business practices. They differed from the Socialist Labor Party in that they stood for reform of the capitalist system, whereas the SLP was dedicated to its overthrow.

Both socialist parties fielded candidates in the 1912 presidential election that put Wilson in the White House. Debs rolled up over a seventh of Wilson's vote, while the Socialist Labor candidate only won three percent of Debs' vote. American socialists clearly preferred reform to revolution.

Debs ran for president in 1900, 1904, 1908, 1912, and 1920, but he never made a strong enough showing to receive any Electoral College votes. His best run was in 1920, after being jailed by Wilson, when he won almost a million votes.

World War I, which brought a communist revolution in Russia, also gave rise to the American Communist Party in 1919. Claiming to represent the interests of workers, farmers, and the lower middle class, the CP was originally affiliated with the Communist International, controlled from Moscow. It won its greatest vote—103,000—in the presidential election of 1932, a year of record unemployment. The CP did not sever its ties with the International until 1940.

The loyalty of all Marxist parties, whether pro- or anti-Soviet, came into question when the New York Legislature expelled five legally elected members of the Socialist Party from its Assembly. This action was reversed as unconstitutional by the Supreme Court in an opinion written by Justice Charles Evans Hughes.

A new Progressive Party arose in 1924, endorsed by the Farmer Labor Party, the Socialist Party, and the American Federation of Labor. Its candidate for president was Senator "Fighting Bob" La Follette, who called for government ownership of railroads and water-power resources; a ban on injunctions against strikes; freedom for farmers and workers to organize and bargain collectively; elimination of child labor; and an end to unlimited powers by private monopolies.

La Follette made an impressive showing against the winning candidate, Republican Calvin Coolidge, scoring almost a third as many votes. It was a record for any third party, broken later only by Governor George Wallace.

From 1928, Socialist Party candidate Norman Thomas ran for five consecutive presidential elections, making him the candidate who had run most frequently in our history.

When the Depression and unemployment plagued Hoover's administration, many third parties pressed their programs as the solution to America's problems. Franklin D. Roosevelt shrewdly undercut all of them by borrowing many of their planks for his own Democratic campaign. He won easily, while six members of the Farmer Labor Party also won congressional seats.

Roosevelt's first-term reforms infuriated ultra-conservatives, who organized the Union Party to oppose his reelection in 1936. Headed by Representative William Lemke, it was endorsed by Rev. Charles E. Coughlin, a powerful "radio priest" whose National Union for Social Justice claimed almost 10 million members. Coughlin peddled Nazi Germany's anti-Semitic propaganda. Urging Lemke's election, he cried out on his radio program, "One thing is sure . . . democracy is doomed! This is our last election. It is fascism or communism. We are at the crossroads. . . . I take the road of fascism!"

Roosevelt received almost 28 million votes and Lemke less than 900,000, but still more than any other third party. Thomas now polled less than 200,000 because most socialists preferred to vote for Roosevelt's popular, liberal New Deal.

Two far-out third-party candidates enlivened the elections of 1956. Henry Krajewski, a tavern owner and former New Jersey pig farmer, ran on the Poor Man's ticket, promising free beer and lower income taxes. His pig emblem mocked the Democratic donkey and Republican elephant. Simon Gould of New York promised to turn America into a meatless society and to abolish war.

The 1960 elections saw a fresh explosion of third parties, each with its own answer to the nation's problems. Joining the scramble for votes were the Socialist Workers' Party, the Socialist Labor Party, the Socialist Workers and Farmers Party of Utah, the Conservative Party of Virginia, the Conservative Party of New Jersey, the Constitution Party, the Constitution Party of Texas, the Prohibition Party, the American Vegetarian Party, the Afro-American Unity Party, the Farmer Labor Party of Iowa, the Industrial Government Party, the Tax Cut Party, the National States Rights Party, the American Third Party, the Greenback Party, and the American Beat Consensus.

The latter party nominated a Chicago bookseller on a platform that promised to abolish the working class, give artists a ten-billion-dollar subsidy, make peace with everybody, and legalize everything. Like most of the third parties, they had little real hope of winning, but they viewed the election process as a way to publicize their ideas and win new followers.

The largest third-party vote that year—almost 228,000—went to the National States Rights Party, which opposed the integration of Southern schools and colleges.

A 1939 meeting of the Michigan branch of the American Communist Party, another prominent third party. PHOTO BY ARTHUR SIEGEL.

"Fighting Bob" La Follette, pictured here in 1910, ran for president as the 1924 Progressive Party candidate. PHOTO COPYRIGHT AMERICAN PRESS ASSOCIATION, 1910.

The Prohibition Party persuaded Congress to adopt the Eighteenth Amendment which banned the sale of liquor and spawned gangster wars over bootlegging in the 1920's. LITHOGRAPH, 1888.

In the 1964 election that saw Lyndon Johnson triumph over Barry Goldwater, the best any third party could do was little better than 21,000 votes for the Socialist Labor candidate.

In 1968, however, a strong new third party arose—the American Independent Party (AIP), which nominated Governor George Wallace of Alabama, a defecting Democrat, for president. The AIP was supported by White Citizens Councils that sprang up in the South in an angry backlash against the Democratic desegregation and civil rights movement. The new party pressed for "law and order," code words for cracking down on civil rights and anti-war demonstrators as well as street crime. Wallace also demanded an end to "control from Washington."

"They say I'm only popular 'cause I'm sayin' what the people want to hear," he declared. "Well, what's wrong with that?" Chomping his cigar in satisfaction, he noted that the segregationists weren't being laughed at anymore. He promised to end federal intervention in Southern civil rights cases and to send "those bureaucrats back to Washington with their briefcases and throw them in the Potomac River. . . . We're gonna show 'em in November that the average American is sick and tired of all these over-educated ivory-tower folks with pointy heads lookin' down their noses at you and me!"

In September, public-opinion polls showed that Wallace was being supported by 20 percent of the voters. Republican candidate Richard Nixon appealed to conservatives not to "waste your vote" on Wallace, since that would only help elect the Democrats. Both major-party candidates held their breath as election results started to pour in.

Because of the AIP's "spoiler" third party, the race was extraordinarily close. The outcome remained in doubt until the following morning. Then Americans learned that Nixon had defeated Hubert Humphrey by only eight tenths of one percent. Wallace's AIP vote reached almost ten million, most of whom would otherwise have voted Democratic, electing Humphrey.

The AIP continued to field a presidential slate in subsequent elections. The party insisted that it was needed to give voters a real choice because "it is common knowledge that the Democratic and the Republican Parties are a farce, and are only two parts of the same political machine—their ideology is the same." The party is strongest in California, its hundred and fifty thousand registered voters making it the largest third party in any state.

The AIP's program calls for local control of schools; a halt to school busing; the election, not appointment, of judges; opposition to handgun control; an end to foreign aid; protective tariffs; strict curbs on immigration; slashed government spending; a return to a gold and silver standard; repeal of the income tax; no government interference in labor unions; less bureaucratic control of the environment; a ban on abortions; withdrawal from the United Nations; a strong military; and vigorous opposition to communist countries. At the same time it opposes stationing American troops in trouble spots abroad.

Party officials are bitter about their treatment by the media. "The AIP has gotten a news blackout and what news coverage we got was not the best," complained G. W. Brown. "Many of our people have bad feelings about the media."

Nevertheless the party succeeded in electing a candidate to the state senate of Tennessee and many others to local government offices in various states. At times the AIP has affiliated with other third parties such as the Conservative Party, the Constitutional Party, and the National American Party, which it broke with in an organizational dispute.

Some states sought to make it almost impossible for a third party to get on the ballot. In Ohio, even though Wallace supporters had gathered over 400,000 signatures on his nominating petition for the 1968 election, they were unable to place his name on the ballot. Ohio's major parties had passed special qualifying laws designed to eliminate third-party and independent candidates.

The case was fought up to the U.S. Supreme Court, which invalidated Ohio's restrictive laws as unconstitutional. In most states now, to qualify for the ballot a candidate needs only five percent as many petition signatures supporting him as there were votes for that office in the previous election.

Attempts to harass left-wing third parties were made by the FBI. For 15 years, starting in 1961, the Socialist Workers Party (SWP) and its affiliated Young Socialist Alliance (YSA) were the targets of electronic surveillance, mail interceptions, forged poison-pen letters, interrogations of members and their families, and scores of break-ins of their homes and offices. During 92 FBI burglaries in a six-year period, the agency photocopied some 10,000 SWP and YSA documents.

Yet when a federal judge demanded that the FBI produce any evidence it had uncovered of "violent revolutionary activity or any other illegal activity" by the SWP or YSA, the FBI had to admit that it had found "absolutely nothing."

The SWP finally sued the FBI for $40 million in damages and demanded an end to any further government harassment. *The New York Times* noted that the FBI then had to admit that the SWP was "a nonviolent Marxist organization committed to running candidates for public office."

Once when a bill had been introduced in Congress to ban the Communist Party, Representative Emanuel Celler of New York pointed out, "If we outlaw the Communist Party, there is no reason why if the Republicans are in control they could not outlaw the Democratic Party. . . . You could say that any party that opposes high tariffs or believes in deficit spending is subversive."

Advocates of keeping *all* third parties legal insist that it is wiser for Americans to hear what they have to say, and to discuss the merit or lack of it of their arguments, rather than have those views circulate illegally where they cannot be confronted. "How will we defeat communism," President Eisenhower once asked, "unless we know what it is, and what it teaches, and why does it have such an appeal for men?"

The Socialist Workers Party stems from the Workingman's Party of 1876. Its Marxist goal is still a classless society based on collective ownership and control of industry and social services. The SWP wants a socialist industrial union government composed of democratically elected representatives from all industries and services. Production would be carried on to satisfy human needs, instead of for profit.

"The same corporations and capitalists who have polluted the air, land, water, and food are the ones who dominate the government and own the politicians who run it," reads the SWP platform. "Government regulatory agencies are bureaucratic wastelands where nothing happens. . . . By 1981 almost 30 million people were living below the official poverty level. Millions more were living just barely above it . . . because the workers who built and operate the nation's economy don't own it. Instead it is owned by a small capitalist class. . . . When its markets are filled, it shuts down production, hurling millions into the ranks of the unemployed."

The party calls for "opposition to the government's war against working people at home and abroad . . . support for the revolutions in Cuba, Nicaragua, Grenada, and El Salvador . . . support for affirmative action and abortion rights . . . for school desegregation . . . for unilateral disarmament of the U.S. military machine." Other demands of the SWP include the Equal Rights Amendment, free college educations, a curb on police brutality, shutting down all nuclear power plants, free medical care, and a secure retirement for all.

The SWP's youth branch, the Young Socialist Alliance, is active on college and high-school campuses. YSA national committee member Lisa Collins explained, "We are leaders in the struggles for Black rights, the rights of women, Latinos, and other oppressed minorities. We work for solidarity with the struggles of workers and oppressed all over the world."

The YSA urged young people to join them in a "Help Wanted" ad that read: "Socialist youth organization needs fighters for a better world. No experience necessary. We guarantee on-the-job training. Work will include participating in the fight for jobs, against racist and sexist discrimination, and against war and union-busting. No pay but very rewarding."

Many third parties feel that the election laws today place them at a disadvantage. Under the Federal Election Campaign Reform Act of 1974, each presidential candidate for the nomination of a major party is eligible to receive federal funds up to $5 million for primary campaigns, and then each major-party nominee is eligible to receive $20 million more for election expenses. Both major parties also receive $2 million each to pay for their national conventions.

Minority parties receive nothing under this law, because not one can meet the difficult eligibility requirements. They see this as a violation of the spirit of free elections.

Third parties also protest their lack of access to the media, while the Democrats and Republicans share equal time. A clause in the Federal Communications Act calls for the media to give fair representation to third-party candidates. But in practice neither the press nor TV gives even a fraction of the time and space allotted to major-party candidates.

Realistically, third parties serve more as gadflies than serious opponents to the Democrats and Republicans, although they may influence a tight election race by diverting votes away from one candidate or the other. The only third-party candidate ever to win the White House was Abraham Lincoln, running on the Republican ticket.

But it was from third parties that Americans first heard about the eight-hour workday, worker's compensation, unemployment insurance, safety codes for working women and children, old-age pensions, public education, public housing, tenement inspections, public health programs, regulation of utilities, and other reforms. Third-party pressure forced the major parties to include many of these demands in their own platforms.

Third parties are vital to our electoral system because they introduce fresh, needed ideas into the political arena, keeping the two major parties from becoming too complacent. They also provide an outlet for protest by those dissatisfied with both the Democrats and Republicans. A high third-party vote sends a message to both major parties.

Significantly, by 1983 only 25 percent of American voters claimed strong ties to a major party, and 33 percent claimed no ties at all. These figures give heart to third-party candidates in their struggle to win over independent voters.

In 1929 Senator William E. Borah, who considered himself a "progressive Republican," told the Senate, "We need not take shelter when someone cries 'Radical!' If measures proposed are unsound, debate will reveal this fact better than anything else that has been discovered in the affairs of government. But if the measures are sound, we want them."

Abraham Flexner, the noted American educator, said, "We must not overlook the important role that extremists play. They are the gadflies that keep society from being too complicated or self-satisfied; they are, if sound, the spearhead of progress."

The day that third parties are no longer allowed to function in American elections will be the day that marks the end of our First Amendment right of dissent.

If you are dissatisfied with the two major parties on a national, state, or local level, investigate which third parties will be on the ballot in the next election. Contact the headquarters of those parties for campaign literature, which will give you a broader base for decision. Your local librarian will be able to help you contact third-party national headquarters.

10

WHAT GOES ON AT POLITICAL CONVENTIONS

Probably the funniest national political conventions ever held were those that took place in 1948, the first to be televised to tens of millions of Americans.

At the Democratic Convention in Philadelphia, its stagers decided to put on a spectacle with pigeons ("doves of peace") sweeping dramatically past a huge floral Liberty Bell during a speech by a committee woman. At a given signal, her chauffeur tried to stir the pigeons out of their hampers. When they refused to fly, he was forced to throw them into the air.

Delegates roared with laughter as the pigeons roosted on perches from which they began soiling the clothes of the dignitaries seated below, who tried to dodge them. When the upset chairman, Speaker of the House Sam Rayburn, banged his gavel for order, one pigeon tried to land on his bald head. He ducked and it landed on his lectern. As he frantically sought to shove it off, the convention fell into hysterics.

Not to be outdone that year, Republicans supporting the nomination of Senator Robert Taft took a huge inflated rubber elephant to their convention to symbolize "Mr. Republican" for the TV cameras. But before the voting began, the elephant began to collapse and sag into a mess of rubber. Some Taft people accused the Democrats of stealing into the convention and sticking a pin in it. Like the elephant, Taft's candidacy also quickly collapsed, and his rival, Thomas Dewey, ran away with the Republican nomination.

If you've ever tuned your TV to a national political convention in progress, you could be forgiven for thinking you were witnessing a carnival. People seem to be going crazy, jumping up and down, tooting horns and shouting, with bands marching around a vast auditorium, drum majorettes dancing, jubilant paraders jiggling signs, streamers flying, balloons soaring. Foreigners witnessing this scene are usually baffled by what all this has to do with elections.

Some sociologists have compared conventions to a form of tribal dancing celebration. The traditional hoopla gives delegates a chance to discharge their high spirits, having fun while going about the serious business of president-making.

While conventions have been criticized as absurd spectacles, the show that they put on has value for the electoral process. It causes millions of voters to tune in and watch, thereby participating vicariously. If the proceedings were devoid of fun and bedlam, most Americans wouldn't watch.

Delegates have usually been middle-class citizens prominent in their community. In 1972, however, the Democrats broke with tradition and sought to make their delegates more representative of the total population. Delegations included students, housewives, blacks, and Hispanics.

The Democrats' rules for delegate selection have since been amended to give professional politicians greater representation once more in each state's contingent. Nevertheless Democratic conventions are still markedly more diverse in composition than those of the Republicans.

The size of a state's population determines how many delegates it is entitled to send to a national convention. About two thirds of the states choose their delegates at their own party conventions. The others hold state primary elections in which all party members can vote directly for delegates pledged to the various candidates.

Each state party determines its own rules for how its delegates may cast their votes at the national convention. Some states hold "winner-take-all" primaries, with the whole state party delegation pledged to vote for the winning candidate. Other states send unpledged delegates, each free to vote for a personal choice. A few states expect delegates to vote whichever way the delegation leader directs.

Still other delegates are pledged to vote for a "favorite son" candidate as president—often their state's governor or senator—for one or two ballots. After that they are freed to shift their votes. If no candidate wins the nomination on the first ballot, a favorite-son candidate may swap his state's support for a political advantage.

At the 1932 Democratic Convention in Chicago, for example, Franklin D. Roosevelt fell short of the two-thirds vote then needed to nominate him. The Texas delegation stood firmly behind their favorite-son candidate, "Cactus Jack" Garner, who was also supported by the California delegation. A deal was then struck by which Garner threw his votes to Roosevelt, cinching FDR's nomination, in return for which Garner was named Roosevelt's choice for vice-president.

Each major party's convention is held in the summer of a presidential election year. The city chosen is usually one with a huge convention hall, lots of hotels, good transportation, and enjoyable recreation facilities. For about a week the attention of the whole nation, and much of the world, is centered upon each party's national convention as it goes about the business of choosing the person who will be one of the two candidates for president of the United States.

Each convention has a credentials committee that "seats" the delegations, ironing out any quarrels over entitlement. At the 1968 Democratic Convention the committee denied seats to the entire Mississippi delegation, on grounds that the state party's procedures for choosing delegates had discriminated against blacks. A rival multi-racial Mississippi delegatation was approved and seated in its place.

After a permanent convention chairman is elected, a prominent party member delivers the keynote speech. The delegates then vote on a party platform drawn up by a platform committee. Its planks usually represent a compromise among various factions within the party who have differing views.

Sometimes the platform so angers one faction that its supporters will walk out of the convention. In actual fact, however, the platform is seldom taken too seriously because the candidate, if elected, usually decides how much of it, if any, he will adhere to during his administration.

By the third or fourth day of the convention, nominations for the presidential candidate begin. Each nominating speech usually ends in a boisterous demonstration, as loud, jubilant, and prolonged as the candidate's supporters can make it. They snake-dance up and down the convention aisles as the band blares.

As shorter seconding speeches are heard, supporters of the candidates scurry around on the convention floor, in side rooms, hotel rooms, and candidates' headquarters, trying to make deals to capture blocs of votes from delegations whose candidates clearly have no chance of being nominated. Little by little, minor candidates are eliminated.

Voting is done verbally, with the states reporting in alphabetical order. A simple majority of the total delegates now elects the nominee in both parties. If the vote is split several ways so that no one candidate wins the required majority, ballot after ballot occurs. The tallies begin to change as minority and favorite-son candidates yield their voting blocs to one leading candidate or another after hasty political deals.

By tradition the presidential nominee gets to name his choice for vice-president. He usually selects someone from a populous state in a different part of the country, where the party ticket needs strengthening. If he is a conservative, he is likely to choose a moderate or liberal vice-president to "balance" the ticket, broadening its appeal. If he is a liberal, his running mate is apt to be moderate or conservative.

State conventions took place before national conventions. During the late 1820's and 1830's, state party conventions were being held all over the country.

"In days gone by, particularly in the nineteenth century, the presidential election was an all-consuming interest for the public," observes historian Jules Abel in his book *The Degradation of the American Presidency.* "It was not a spectator interest. . . . It was an event for mass participation in parades, torchlight processions, meetings, and barbecues, not only for adults, but for teenage boys and girls. There was endless speech-making and discussion. Contemporary observers noted

National conventions today are considerably more lavish than they were at the time of the 1860 Republican Convention, pictured here. WOOD ENGRAVING FROM *HARPER'S WEEKLY*, 1860.

Despite the bedlam, the delegates at a convention are usually prominent middle-class citizens. Democrats, beginning in 1972, sought to include more diverse representation.

The merrymaking at national conventions has been compared by sociologists to a tribal dancing celebration of sorts. The scene on the left is of the 1888 Democratic Convention in St. Louis. REPRODUCTION OF ENGRAVING BY WOODWARD & TIERNAN IN NATIONAL DEMOCRATIC CONVENTION.

that the carnival proceedings provided an emotional outlet and even communal recreation for the masses, at a time when there was little else available that would give the same emotional release or stimulus."

The first national party convention was called by the Anti-Mason Party in Philadelphia in 1830, to defeat a second term for Andrew Jackson. Two years later the Democrats and National Republicans held nominating conventions of their own.

The conventions provided galleries where the public could enjoy the spectacle and join in yelling enthusiastically for their favorite candidates. At the 1860 Republican Convention in Chicago, William H. Seward emerged as the front-runner for the presidential nomination. Reacting swiftly, Abraham Lincoln's campaign manager counterfeited admission tickets and used them to pack the galleries with Lincoln supporters. As they kept yelling his name to stampede the convention, Lincoln aides scooted around the floor making deals for votes. Lincoln won on the third ballot.

The 1896 Democratic Convention, also in Chicago, brought about the first real political class struggle in the nation. The nomination was wide open until the relatively unknown "Boy Orator of the River Platte," thirty-six-year-old William Jennings Bryan, made his famous Cross of Gold speech attacking Eastern bankers on behalf of America's poor debtor class.

"The delegates arose and marched for an hour, shouting, weeping, rejoicing," poet-reporter Edgar Lee Masters related. "They lifted this orator upon their shoulders and carried him as if he had been a god. At last a man!" The delegates shouted themselves hoarse crying his name, and he was nominated on the fourth ballot.

Worried, Republican Party boss Mark Hanna wrote to his presidential choice, William McKinley, "The Chicago convention has changed everything. . . . I consider the situation in the West quite alarming as business is going to pieces and idle men will multiply rapidly. With this communistic spirit abroad the cry of 'free silver' will be catching."

When the Republican Convention met, it fascinated a Russian visitor, M. I. Ostrogorski, who witnessed it. "As soon as the aspirant's name is uttered," he reported, "the delegates who support him and the paid applauders jump up on their seats and break into cheers. . . . It is enough for the claque to give the signal for the [crowd] to go into convulsions. . . . [The candidate's] portrait . . . is hoisted aloft and carried about the hall, everyone is on his legs, shouting, screaming, tossing hats and handkerchiefs into the air, waving small flags and open umbrellas. It is a sort of pandemonium or Bedlam. . . . The crowd does not stop until compelled by fatigue, by exhaustion." The popularity of the candidates was judged by how long the demonstrations for them lasted.

Ostrogorski took a dim view of the American way: "You realize what a colossal travesty of popular institutions you have just been witnessing. A greedy crowd of office-holders, or of office-seekers, disguised as delegates of the people . . . indulged in . . . intrigues and maneuvers, the object of which was the chief magistracy of the greatest Republic."

In those unsophisticated days it was easier for state party bosses to handpick delegates and manipulate conventions. Robert White noted in his book *American Government: Democracy at Work* that when the 1896 Cook County Convention was held in Chicago to select delegates to the Democratic National Convention, some 89 percent of those chosen were either ex-convicts, saloonkeepers, persons previously tried for murder, vagrants, ex-prizefighters, gamblers, or political employees.

One of the most colorful years for national conventions was 1912. At the Republican Convention in Chicago, supporters of William Howard Taft and Theodore Roosevelt clashed when the Taft forces stacked the convention with 74 delegates whose credentials were challenged by the Roosevelt forces.

When Taft supporter Elihu Root was named convention chairman, ruling in favor of Taft, Roosevelt supporters jeered this "railroading" by yelling, "Toot! Toot! All aboard! Choo choo!" Sandpaper was rubbed to imitate the noises of a train.

As Senator Warren Harding of Ohio rose to nominate Taft, fistfights broke out. Angry Roosevelt delegates stormed out of the hall when Taft was renominated. One month later they staged a Progressive Party convention to nominate Roosevelt.

The split in Republican ranks assured the election of whichever Democratic candidate was nominated. When the Democrats met in Baltimore, party bosses had decided to nominate House Speaker Champ

The National Republican Party of the United States,

Assembled in National Convention, in the City of Chicago, on the twentieth day of May, 1868, make the following

DECLARATION OF PRINCIPLES:

First. — We congratulate the country on the assured success of the reconstruction policy of Congress, as evinced by the adoption, by a majority of the States lately in rebellion, of constitutions securing equal civil and political rights to all. It is the duty of the government to sustain these institutions, and to prevent the people of such States from being remitted to a state of anarchy.

Second. — The guarantee by Congress of equal suffrage to all loyal men at the South was demanded by every consideration of public safety, of gratitude, and of justice, and must be maintained. The whole question of suffrage in all the loyal States properly belongs to the people of those States.

Third. — We denounce all forms of repudiation as a national crime; and declare that the national honor requires the payment of the public indebtedness, in the utmost good faith, to all creditors at home and abroad, not only according to the letter, but to the spirit, of the law under which it was contracted.

Fourth. — It is due to the labor of the nation that taxation shall be equalized and reduced as rapidly as the national faith shall permit.

Fifth. — The national debt, contracted as it has been for the preservation of the Union for all time to come, should be extended over a fair period for redemption; and it is the duty of Congress to reduce the rate of interest thereon whenever it can be honestly done.

Sixth. — The best policy to diminish our burden of debt is to so improve our credit that capitalists will seek to loan us money at lower rates of interest than we now pay, and must continue to pay so long as repudiation, partial or total, open or covert, is threatened or suspected.

Seventh. — The government of the United States should be administered with the strictest economy; and the corruptions which have been so shamefully nursed and fostered by Andrew Johnson call loudly for a radical reform.

Eighth. — We professedly deplore the untimely and tragic death of Abraham Lincoln, and regret the accession of Andrew Johnson to the presidency; who has acted treacherously to the people who elected him, and the cause he was pledged to support; who has usurped high legislative and judicial functions; who has refused to execute the laws; who has used his high office to induce other officers to ignore and violate the laws; who has employed his executive powers to render insecure the property, the peace, the liberty, and the life of the citizen; who has abused the pardoning power; who has denounced the national legislature as unconstitutional; who has persistently and corruptly resisted, by every measure in his power, every proper attempt at the

reconstruction of the States lately in rebellion; who has perverted the public patronage into an engine of wholesale corruption; and who has justly been impeached for high crimes and misdemeanors, and properly pronounced guilty thereof by a vote of thirty-five senators.

Ninth. — The doctrine of Great Britain and other European powers, that because a man is once a subject he is always so, must be resisted at every hazard by the United States as a relic of feudal times, not authorized by the law of nations, and at war with our national honor and independence. Naturalized citizens are entitled to be protected in all their rights of citizenship as though they were native born; and no citizen of the United States, native or naturalized, must be liable to arrest and imprisonment by any foreign power for acts done or words spoken in this country; and if they are so arrested and imprisoned, it is the duty of the government to interfere in their behalf.

Tenth. — Of all who were faithful in the trials of the late war, there were none entitled to more special honor than the brave soldiers and seamen who endured the hardships of campaign and cruise, and imperilled their lives in the service of the country. The bounties and pensions provided by the laws for these brave defenders, are obligations never to be forgotten; the widows and orphans of the gallant dead are the wards of the people, a sacred legacy bequeathed to the nation's fostering care.

Eleventh. — Foreign immigration, which in the past has added so much to the wealth, development and resources, and the increase of power to this nation, the asylum of the oppressed of all nations, should be fostered and encouraged by a liberal and just policy.

Twelfth. — This Convention declares itself in sympathy with all the oppressed peoples which are struggling for their rights.

Thirteenth. — We highly commend the spirit of magnanimity and forgiveness with which men who have served in the rebellion, but now frankly and honestly co-operate with us in restoring peace to the country, and in reconstructing the Southern State governments upon the basis of impartial justice and equal rights, are received back into the communion of the loyal people, and are in favor of the removal of the disqualifications and restrictions imposed upon the late rebels in the same measure as their spirit of loyalty will direct, and as may be consistent with the safety of the people.

Fourteenth. — We recognize the great principles laid down in the immortal Declaration of Independence as the true foundations of democratic government, and we hail with gladness every effort towards making these principles a living reality on every inch of American soil.

SURRENDER OF VICKSBURG.   THE CAPITOL.   SURRENDER OF GENERAL LEE.

The Republican platform of 1868. Platforms are seldom taken too seriously, because the candidate decides how much of it he or she will adhere to once elected. WOODCUT PRINTED BY A. HOLLAND, COPYRIGHT 1868

Clark of Missouri, who held a commanding lead in ballot after ballot. Woodrow Wilson's campaign manager, William McCombs, begged him to make a deal with New York's corrupt Tammany political machine for their 90 votes.

Wilson refused. On the tenth ballot, Clark had a 200-vote lead over Wilson. His managers decided to stampede the convention with a long, noisy Clark demonstration. But while this was going on, Wilson's aides ran around the hall urging his delegates to hold fast. They did. Had Clark's aides not given the Wilson forces time to rally their delegates, Clark might have won on a fast eleventh ballot.

The struggle went on for four days and thirteen ballots. In desperation Clark made a deal with Tammany for their votes. When William Jennings Bryan learned of it, he rose angrily to declare that since "sinister forces" were now supporting Clark, he intended to throw his support to Wilson.

The convention fell into an uproar. In the next three days Wilson's vote mounted steadily until he was finally nominated on the forty-sixth ballot.

A new dimension to the art of manipulating a presidential convention was developed by Senator John F. Kennedy in 1960. He posted spies in every state delegation to relay sentiment there, with hour by hour checks of every change and daily reports on each delegate's voting intentions. Kennedy's brother Robert had 23 phones at Kennedy headquarters, all busy pressuring delegates in opposition camps to switch over.

Perhaps the stormiest convention in history was the 1968 Democratic convention in Chicago, when protests against the Vietnam War resulted in brutal attacks by Chicago police against anti-war demonstrators. When delegates became aware of what was going on in Chicago's streets, Senator Abraham Ribicoff of Connecticut furiously deviated from his speech to the convention to denounce the Chicago police as "gestapo."

TV cameras caught Chicago's enraged Mayor Daley shouting obscenities at Ribicoff. The next day, Daley packed the galleries with his patronage workers, who chanted on cue, "We love Daley, we love Daley!" On signal they whooped it up for him throughout the evening.

When the New Hampshire delegation tried to protest the arrest of their chairman by Daley's police, they were drowned out by the roar of Daley's claque.

Jubilant Republicans demanded, "How can the Democrats bring order to the country if they can't even bring order to their own convention?" The riotous Democratic convention doomed the chances of its nominee, Hubert Humphrey.

But it enabled the peace forces of Senator George McGovern to reduce the role of party bosses at the next Democratic convention, in 1972. This convention was probably more representative of rank-and-file Democrats than any other ever held. McGovern easily won the nomination, only to lose every state but one in the national election.

As a rule the weakness of the convention system is that all too frequently each party nominates a presidential candidate who is such a compromise of conflicting interests within the party that he is a mediocre, uninspiring choice. The electorate is then faced with a choice between what they often see as Tweedledum and Tweedledee. Even though third parties offer alternative candidates, when the chips are down most voters play safe, voting for a major-party candidate.

If a major party nominates a candidate who takes a bold stand on controversial issues, like McGovern in 1972, it is likely to suffer a devastating defeat. Political wisdom decrees that most voters are middle-of-the-road. Thus our conventions tend to nominate candidates who appeal largely to moderate voters. Democrats generally nominate a somewhat liberal candidate, like Jimmy Carter, while Republicans choose a somewhat conservative candidate, like Ronald Reagan.

America will have to be faced with a desperate dilemma before voters will be given a major-party choice between extreme left- or right-wing presidential candidates.

11

HOT AIR AND COLD TURKEY ON THE CAMPAIGN TRAIL

A leather-lunged politician campaigning for the Senate cried out to a crowd in ringing tones, "I want you to know that I hate communism, socialism, atheism, Marxism—*and every other* ism *in the world!*"

"What!" shouted a straight-faced heckler. "Do you expect all of us here to vote for a man who comes right out and says he hates capital*ism* and American*ism?*"

When candidates hit the campaign trail, most of them try to give the impression that they are talking cold turkey to their constituents. Often, however, their sentiments come across more like hot air. There is widespread skepticism about the factual content of candidates' assertions and about the validity of the promises they make.

Voters also sprinkle liberally with salt the charges and countercharges candidates fling at each other. Some candidates find it more effective simply to laugh off a rival's accusations. Attacked, one mayoral candidate replied blandly, "There are no depths, apparently, to which my opponent will not rise." The subtle joke brought laughter and applause.

Becoming a political candidate requires a peculiar combination of pride and humility. One must consider oneself eminent enough to be elected to govern others, yet humble enough to plead for votes. As historian Jules Abel noted, "It is certainly undignified for a man who will be

President of the United States to be darting in and out of drugstores, supermarkets, and beauty shops clasping hands."

For that reason, early presidential candidates in our history did not campaign. The election contest that first introduced campaigns, complete with raucous rallies, torchlight parades, campaign songs, and windy speeches, occurred in 1832, when Andrew Jackson ran against Henry Clay. "God help the nation!" wrote one observer. "I am afraid it will run mad."

Windy political speeches became labeled "bunk" as the result of an 1821 session of Congress, which was forced to twiddle its thumbs on an important bill because Representative Felix Walker of North Carolina insisted upon making an endless speech on behalf of his constituents back home in Buncombe County. After pleas and groans failed to shut him up, Congress immortalized him by labeling all such political prattle "buncombe," which soon became shortened to simply "bunk."

If candidates can, on the campaign trail they will duck or straddle controversial issues when endorsing one side means losing votes on the other. When the first Adlai E. Stevenson was campaigning as the Democratic vice-presidential candidate in 1892, he showed a touch of genius in the art of waffling on a ticklish issue. Touring the Northwest in a campaign train, he became aware that a hot battle was raging over whether to name the region's highest mountain Mt. Rainier or Mt. Tacoma. He was pressed at each stop to name his choice.

Speaking from the rear train platform, Stevenson would end each speech by saying, "I pledge myself, here and now, that if elected I will not rest until this glorious mountain is properly named—." At that point he would pull a cord and the engineer would blow his whistle, drowning out Stevenson's choice as the train chuffed out of the station.

President Martin Van Buren was so careful not to take any stand in his political speeches that a story circulated about his being asked if he agreed that the sun rose in the east. Van Buren supposedly replied, "I presume the fact is according to the common impression, but as I sleep until after sunrise, I cannot speak from my own knowledge."

When Van Buren ran for reelection in 1840, it was Horace Greeley who brought campaigning to the height of absurdity. Greeley masterminded the campaign of Van Buren's Whig opponent, William Henry

Harrison, a former Indian fighter who had won the obscure battle of Tippecanoe 29 years earlier. Since there were few real issues in the election, Greeley decided to invent a personality issue.

He publicized the Harrison-Tyler ticket with a nonsensical slogan, "Tippecanoe and Tyler, too!" and stirred emotions with rallies, cannon fire, fireworks, torchlight parades, and campaign songs. *("What has caused this great commotion-motion-motion, Our country through? It is the ball a-rollin' on—for Tippecanoe and Tyler, too!")* Parading men pushed huge balls taller than themselves. The nation waved Tippecanoe flags, wore Tippecanoe badges, blew their noses in Tippecanoe handkerchiefs, washed with Tippecanoe soap. Every town had its Tippecanoe club and chorus.

A whisper campaign by Whigs accused Van Buren of being a fop who sprayed his whiskers with French eau de cologne, who slept in a King Louis XV bed, who ate French food from silver plates, and who rode in a British-made gilt coach.

Stung, one Democratic journalist sneered that if old Tippecanoe were given $2,000 and a jug of hard cider, he'd be happier in a log cabin than in the White House. Greeley gleefully seized on this admission that the Whig candidate was a Davy Crockett type. He flooded the country with log-cabin badges, songs, and clubs and even log cabins on wheels where thirsty voters could toast old Tippecanoe with hard cider.

"We could meet the Whigs on the field of argument and beat them without effort," complained an editorial in the Democratic *New York Evening Post.* "But when they lay down the weapons of argument and attack us with musical notes, what can we do?" After old Tippecanoe was elected, politician Philip Hone observed that he'd been "sung into the presidency."

Greeley later expressed regrets for his part in "bamboozling" the American people, and broke with the Whig Party he had helped put in office. But the example he set was not lost on politicians. Ever since, election campaigns have been enlivened by lots of music, parades, souvenirs, stunts, and hoopla to whip up enthusiasm for candidates.

When Greeley himself ran for president in 1872 on the Democratic and Liberal Republican tickets against the corrupt Grant administration, his campaign theme was: "Turn the rascals out!" Grant's forces lampooned Greeley as a wild, inconsistent, impulsive, impractical dreamer who would plunge the nation into chaos. When only six states—all Southern—had given Greeley their electoral votes, his defeat was humiliating.

"I am the worst beaten man that ever ran for high office," he told his daughters gloomily. "And I have been assailed so bitterly that I hardly know now whether I was running for the presidency or the penitentiary!"

Dirty campaigning is marked by last-minute slanders aimed at damaging a candidate just before voters go to the polls, when it is too late for an effective answer. In 1844 James Polk's political enemies waited until the last moment to circulate a false document accusing him of buying and branding a slave.

In 1884 Republicans charged Grover Cleveland with having fathered a child out of wedlock. They paraded up New York's Fifth Avenue taunting, "Ma, Ma, where's my Pa?" The Democrats had time to shape up a quick counter-parade yelling the answer, "Gone to the White House—ha-ha-ha!" And Cleveland did go.

In this century an amusing technique to slur a political opponent was invented in a 1950 Florida senatorial campaign by George Smathers. He thundered that Senator Claude Pepper's sister was a "thespian," his brother a "practicing Homo sapiens," and that at college Pepper had openly "matriculated."

Uneducated voters who didn't understand these terms assumed that they were shocking disclosures. When Pepper lost the election, he could hardly blame Smathers for accusing him of having a sister who was an actress and a brother who was human, and of having been enrolled in a college.

Professional politicians expect candidates to spout a lot of hot air, but they are sometimes dismayed when a candidate they support turns out to mean what he says. New Jersey's political boss, Democrat "Sugar Jim" Smith, wasn't ruffled in 1910 when he read an article by Woodrow Wilson that declared, "The boss—a man elected by no votes . . . makes himself a veritable tyrant among us, and seems to cheat us of self-government."

Wilson had entered the governor's race and had widespread support. Smith's lieutenant, Bob Davis, was asked whether he thought Wilson would make a good governor. "How the devil do I know?" he growled. "He'll make a good *candidate*, and that's all that interests me!" But before Wilson could get the Democratic machine behind him, he had to promise Smith not to interfere with it if he were elected.

Wilson astonished Smith by refusing to spend a penny more than necessary on his campaign, even returning some contributions as unnecessary. He perplexed the political boss further by making fun of himself in campaign speeches.

When the Republicans opposed him with a handsome candidate who referred to Wilson as ugly, Wilson evoked roars of laughter from crowds with a satire of himself he'd written:

> *For beauty I am not a star,*
> *There are hundreds more handsome by far,*
> > *But my face, I don't mind it,*
> > *For I am behind it;*
> *It's the people in front that I jar!*

In his campaign Wilson promised voters to end the power of political bosses in New Jersey. Boss Smith merely smiled at such vote-getting rhetoric. But after Wilson's election, when Smith decided to become a state senator, the new governor prevented it. Smith was outraged.

"The governor has given striking evidence," he snarled, "of his aptitude in the art of foul play."

From across the river in New York came indignant agreement from another political boss, Tammany Hall's Richard Croker. "An ingrate is no good in politics!" he thundered.

But Wilson had his own political code of honor. He displayed his integrity when he ran for president against Theodore Roosevelt and William Howard Taft in 1912. Three weeks before election day, while Roosevelt was speaking to a crowd in Milwaukee, a fanatic shot him at almost point-blank range. The bullet punctured his rib, but the bloodied candidate insisted upon continuing with his speech. "I do not care a rap about being shot," he growled. "Not a rap!"

Admiring Roosevelt's courage, Wilson showed gentlemanly restraint, unusual in politics, by halting his campaign until his opponent had recovered. The country admired his sportsmanship and ended up putting him in the White House.

But Wilson proved less than generous as president toward a third-party candidate who dared criticize his decision to take the United States into World War I "to save the world for democracy." In 1918 socialist candidate Eugene Debs denounced the war as a capitalist scramble for markets. "I am opposed," he declared, "to every war but one . . . the worldwide war of social revolution." Furious, Wilson saw to it that Debs was arrested and sentenced to ten years in prison.

From behind bars in 1920, Convict 9653 ran for president against Republican Warren Harding and Democrat James Cox. Debs appealed to voters to think deeply about the issues, declaring, "I would rather have a man think and vote against me than give me his vote like a sheep!" Although Harding was elected, almost a million Americans voted for Convict 9653.

There were two ironic aftermaths to Debs's imprisonment. When Wilson toured America pleading for support to U.S. entry into the League of Nations, his argument was an echo of the very one he had jailed Debs for presenting earlier.

"The real reason that the war . . . took place," he then admitted, "was that Germany was afraid her commercial rivals were going to get the better of her, and . . . they thought Germany would get the commercial advantage of them." Yet Wilson still refused to pardon Debs for having told that truth.

The second irony was that Wilson, a professed liberal, was the president who kept Debs behind bars while Harding, a conservative Republican, was the president who issued the socialist firebrand a pardon.

The first time Americans heard campaign speeches over the radio was in 1924, during the election race between Republican Calvin Coolidge and Democrat John W. Davis, with Progressive/Socialist candidate Robert M. La Follette challenging both.

The Republicans won handily with their slogan "Keep Cool with Coolidge," although La Follette won almost 5 million votes, over half as much as the Democratic total.

A notable governor's contest took place in South Dakota in 1926. William J. Bular delighted voters with what has to be the most wonderfully candid campaign in election history.

"There are no issues," he declared bluntly. "My opponent has a job and I want it. That's what this election is about." Such unabashed honesty made him governor of South Dakota.

Another delicious campaign occurred that year in the North Carolina Democratic primary for senator, when Robert Reynolds defeated incumbent Senator Cameron Morrison by holding up a jar of caviar and blaring, "Cam eats fish eggs, and Red Russian fish eggs at that, and they cost two dollars. Do you want a senator who ain't too high and mighty to eat good old North Carolina hen eggs, or don't you?"

One of the worst hate campaigns was mounted against Democrat Al Smith in the 1928 presidential race with Republican Herbert Hoover, who subsequently promised to put "a chicken in every pot and a car in every garage." Scurrilous campaign literature accused Smith of favoring interracial marriage and seeking to put the White House under control of the Vatican. The six-million vote margin of his defeat was so severe that no other Roman Catholic candidate was nominated for president until Kennedy, 32 years later.

Hoover's election, however, turned out disastrously for the Republican Party. A severe economic depression beginning in 1929 required drastic corrective measures. In 1932 Democrat Franklin D. Roosevelt's campaign insisted that only total federal planning—a New Deal for the "forgotten man"—could provide jobs for 15 million unemployed workers.

Hoover denounced Roosevelt's New Deal as "a promise no government can fulfill . . . a proposal of revolutionary changes that would undermine and destroy the fundamentals of the American system."

This election contest saw the first airplane used in a political campaign, when Roosevelt flew from the governor's mansion in Albany to Chicago to accept the Democratic nomination. From then on, most major presidential candidates used air travel to meet their speaking commitments.

Despite Roosevelt's election, the economic crisis in the 1930's brought out a proliferation of third-party and independent candidates with radical solutions for the nation's ills. Dr. Francis E. Townsend of California won followers with his Townsend Plan to end the Depression by paying every American over 60 the sum of $200 a month to be spent the same month, thus providing a business stimulus. This general idea was co-opted by Roosevelt in his Social Security program.

Senator Huey "Kingfish" Long of Louisiana unveiled his "Share the Wealth" program ("Every man a king!"). He promised every American a $6,000 homestead allowance, a $2,500 income, a car, and a radio. "Of course we can have Fascism in this country," he said, "but we'll have to call it anti-Fascism."

But all third-party candidates were decisively defeated by Roosevelt. Most Americans were suspicious of radical solutions, preferring to trust the programs of the more liberal of the two major political parties.

The heated political climate, however, allowed some far-out candidates to win election with bizarre rhetoric.

In Mississippi, demagogue Theodore Bilbo won a U.S. Senate seat by haranguing crowds with a list of the people and institutions he opposed. These included "farmer murderers, poor-folk haters, shooters of widows and orphans, international well-poisoners, charity hospital destroyers, spitters on our heroic veterans, rich enemies of our public schools, private bankers . . . unemployment makers, pacifists, communists, munition manufacturers, and skunks who steal Gideon Bibles." He was elected again and again.

Most Americans were less gullible. When Roosevelt ran for reelection in 1936, his Republican opponent, Alf Landon, told an Albuquerque audience, "Franklin D. Roosevelt proposes to destroy the right to elect your own representatives, to talk politics on street corners, to march in political parades, to attend the church of your own faith, to be tried by jury, and to own property." New Deal enthusiasts laughed. FDR was voted back into office by every state with the rock-ribbed Republican exceptions of Maine and Vermont.

The Roosevelt thirties saw the rise of some American sympathizers with Adolf Hitler's Nazi Germany. Organized in such groups as the Christian Front, the German-American Bund, and Defenders of the Christian Faith, they denounced Roosevelt as a communist. The Defenders' leader, Rev. Gerald B. Winrod of Wichita, Kansas, claimed 100,000 followers. Seeking the Republican nomination for senator in 1938, he labeled the Catholic Church "the harlot of the Bible" and called the

Democrat and Roman Catholic Al Smith was the object of a hate campaign by Republican presidential candidate Herbert Hoover in 1928. Smith was accused of seeking to put the White House under control of the Vatican. PHOTO BY UNDERWOOD & UNDERWOOD.

When Eugene Debs denounced President Woodrow Wilson for entering World War I, Wilson had him sentenced to ten years in prison. Debs was later pardoned by President Warren Harding, against whom he had run for office from prison.

moderate National Association for the Advancement of Colored People (NAACP) "a black nest of Reds."

William Allen White, respected editor of the *Emporia Gazette*, warned fellow Kansans, "To nominate him, we must defend his position as a peddler of racial and religious hatred—a Nazi position." Kansans rebuffed Winrod in the primary.

Popular though he was, Roosevelt was not above some political chicanery when he sought to break presidential tradition by seeking a third term. To give the impression that Roosevelt was only responding to an imperative draft, Chicago's Superintendent of Sewers, Thomas McGary, was hidden in the basement of the convention hall with a microphone connected to the convention loudspeaker. For 22 minutes he kept yelling, "We want Roosevelt!" until all the delegates joined in, touching off a wild demonstration on the floor.

The Republicans were desperate to stop a fourth term for Roosevelt. Seeking an issue to oust him, their candidate, New York Governor Thomas Dewey, accused the president of having ordered a U.S. Navy destroyer to the Aleutians just to pick up his dog Fala, which had been left behind.

Roosevelt shrewdly boomeranged the attack with humor, declaring, "These Republican leaders have not been content with attacks upon me, or my wife or my sons—they now include my little dog Fala. Unlike the members of my family, he resents this. Being a Scottie, as soon as he learned that the Republican fiction writers had concocted a story that I . . . had sent a destroyer back to find him at a cost to the taxpayers of two or three or twenty million dollars, his Scotch soul was furious. He has not been the same dog since!"

Dewey suffered a further setback when a news photographer snapped him from the side of a stage. The photo showed the small, stiff-looking candidate standing on two cardboard cartons in order to have his head reach above the lectern.

Reporters also had a field day when Alice Roosevelt Longworth, Teddy's daughter and a celebrated figure in Washington, expressed her opinion of Dewey. "How can you vote," she asked wryly, "for a man who looks like the bridegroom on a wedding cake?"

Demolished by Roosevelt, Dewey tried again in 1948 against Harry S Truman. The unlucky candidate made another mistake while campaigning by train through the Midwest. One day the engineer mistook a signal and pulled the train out of the station while Dewey was still speaking from the rear platform.

"That lunatic!" Dewey exclaimed. "He ought to be shot at sunrise! But we'll let him off this time." These remarks, quoted widely in the press, cost him millions of labor votes.

Truman, in turn, antagonized many Southern voters by pledging to ask Congress for a new civil rights act to give voting power to Southern blacks. Some 6,000 Southern delegates bolted the Democratic Party. Reporters pointed out to the Southerners' own presidential candidate, South Carolina Governor J. Strom Thurmond, that Truman was simply pursuing policies advocated by Roosevelt. "I agree," Thurmond replied testily, "but Truman really *means* it!"

Some presidential candidates have not hesitated to use below-the-belt tactics to achieve their ambition to sit in the White House. Richard M. Nixon manifested this ability from the very beginning of his political career.

When he first ran for Congress in California, his campaign manager, Murray Chotiner, taught him how to use untrue charges to keep his opponent off balance. With Cold War hysteria rampant in America after World War II, Nixon falsely accused his Democratic opponent of "voting the Moscow line in Congress." He won the election.

In 1950 Nixon campaigned for a Senate seat against Democratic Congresswoman Helen Gahagan Douglas. Labeling her "the Pink Lady," he charged, "During five years in Congress, Helen Douglas voted 353 times exactly as has Vito Marcantonio, the notorious communist party-line Congressman from New York."

Outraged, Douglas replied, "Although Mr. Nixon is a Republican, he voted 112 times the same way Marcantonio did. I voted 85 percent of the time with a majority of either the House or my party. I am not a communist." But just before election day, Nixon and Chotiner distributed over half a million bright pink leaflets repeating the same slur. Douglas was defeated, and Richard Nixon went to the Senate.

Years later, seeking to shed the nickname "Tricky Dickie," Nixon apologized for the smear of Helen Douglas. "I'm sorry about that epi-

Republican Thomas Dewey was defeated by both FDR and Truman. The media picked up on his physical shortcomings and a belittling comment that he directed at the engineer of his campaign train.

Richard Nixon, here at his 1969 inauguration, consistently tried to portray his Democratic opponents, in various elections, as communists.

sode," he said plaintively, explaining, "I was a very young man." But in his campaigns he persisted in trying to pin a Red label on Democratic opponents. Eminent journalist Walter Lippmann described him as a "ruthless partisan . . . who divides and embitters people."

During Nixon's 1952 campaign for the vice-presidency on the Republican ticket with Eisenhower, the *New York Post* revealed that wealthy California bankers had provided him with a secret slush fund. Their spokesman explained frankly, "Dick did just what we wanted him to do." Shocked aides of Eisenhower urged him to drop Nixon from the ticket.

Nixon accused communists of trying to smear him, but Eisenhower compelled him to go on TV to convince voters that he was "clean as a hound's tooth." If he failed, he would be dropped, his political career finished. In his famous televised "Checkers" speech, Nixon denied using the slush fund for his personal use or doing favors for his wealthy backers.

Pointing out that his wife, Pat, had no mink coat but only a "respectable Republican cloth coat," he said he had accepted only one personal gift—his cocker spaniel, Checkers. He appealed to millions of dog lovers with a sentimental account of how much his children loved Checkers, so that "regardless of what they say about it, we're going to keep it."

Variety, the show-business weekly, called the Nixon telecast a soap opera—"a slick production" aimed at plucking the heartstrings of the unsophisticated. But it worked. Nixon was kept in the campaign, his career saved.

When Eisenhower decided to campaign in the Democratic "solid South," his advisers protested it would just be a waste of time and money. But the South proved to have plenty of "Citizens for Eisenhower" clubs. They turned out enthusiastically at all whistle-stops of his campaign train, even after midnight, when Ike would appear on the rear platform, yawning in his dressing gown, with his wife, Mamie, in robe and curlers.

Campaigning in Wisconsin, home state of then-powerful Senator Joe McCarthy, Eisenhower told him bluntly, "I'm going to make it clear that I oppose your un-American methods of combatting communism."

McCarthy sneered, "If you say that, you'll be booed."

Ike retorted, "I'll gladly be booed for standing for my own conception of justice!" And he did tell crowds that if elected, he would oppose McCarthy's practice of slandering people as Communists.

Eisenhower proved such a popular campaigner that the Republican National Committee kept him traveling and speaking seven days a week, with only five hours of sleep a night. "Are they trying to perform the feat," he moaned, "of electing a dead man?" He admitted he often asked himself, "What the dickens are *you* doing here, Eisenhower?" He once sighed, "If the people don't want me, that doesn't matter. . . . I've got a heck of a lot of fishing I'll be happy to do!"

The Republicans introduced a new campaign tactic, following Democratic candidate Adlai Stevenson wherever he went with a "Truth Squad" that rebutted him in the local media.

After Eisenhower won a landslide victory, the two candidates faced each other again in 1956. When his Republican advisers urged him to indulge in some campaign hyperbole, Ike refused, telling them, "There's no use my making compromises with the truth, supposedly for the party, because if I were caught in one falsehood, and what I stand for in people's eyes got tarnished, then not just me but the whole Republican gang would be finished!"

Poor Stevenson was almost drowned out by cries of "I like Ike!" Smiling bravely, he would concede, "I like Ike, too, but not his policies."

Eisenhower refused to listen to Stevenson's speeches. "It's not going to do me any good to study what that monkey's saying," he snapped, "since I have no intention of answering him anyway!"

Voters gave him a near-record plurality of almost 10 million votes, a tremendous personal triumph. But he could not transfer his personal magic to the entire Republican ticket. The Democrats captured both houses of Congress.

Eisenhower was a sincere candidate, but he was not without a touch of political cynicism. Shown a speech written for him by Emmet John Hughes of his staff, he scowled that he wanted "a few more 'cheer' lines in this speech. 'Cause a mob like this doesn't want to think—they just want to yowl."

John F. Kennedy and his brother Ted, sons of a wealthy father, had to face insinuations that his millions were being poured into their campaigns to "buy them elections." Both brothers chose to reply tongue in cheek.

At a political dinner of New Yorkers supporting John F. Kennedy's presidential candidacy, he read out a pretended telegram from his father: "Dear Jack: Don't buy one vote more than necessary. I'll be damned if I pay for a landslide!"

Campaigning for the Senate in 1962, Ted Kennedy also drew roars of laughter by telling of speaking at a factory where one worker angrily accused him of never having had to work a day in his life. "Afterward," Kennedy joked, "another worker came up to me and said, 'Let me tell you something, son—you ain't missed a thing!'"

In the 1964 election the Democrats sought to portray Republican presidential candidate Barry Goldwater as a right-wing extremist who might unleash a nuclear war with the Soviet Union. They broadcast a TV commercial showing a little girl with a daisy dissolving in a cloud of atomic dust, as President Lyndon Johnson described the consequences of people not loving each other. The allusion to Goldwater was clear.

Republican Senator Thruston Morton of Kentucky raged against "President Johnson's efforts over national television . . . to win the election by scaring the wits out of the children in order to pressure their parents." Many Democrats were equally offended; Vice-President Hubert Humphrey called the controversial commercial "unfortunate." It was withdrawn, but Goldwater's image as a warmonger lingered. Johnson was elected by a huge majority.

One of the most difficult campaigns in American history was waged by Hubert Humphrey in 1968 after the split in Democratic ranks because of his support of the Vietnam War. While Nixon drew 100,000 people to a Chicago rally, a few days later in Philadelphia only 10,000 turned out to listen to Humphrey. And many hecklers booed and jeered, shouting "Sellout!" and "Shame!" at the once respected liberal.

When his running mate, Ed Muskie, was similarly drowned out by a crowd of angry college students, he offered their leader ten minutes at his microphone to air their grievances, if they would then agree to listen to his reply. The students cheered him and accepted the offer.

Late in the campaign, Humphrey desperately broke with the president on his discredited war policy, but by then it was too late. Liberals refused to forgive him. As the campaign grew hot down to the wire, Humphrey taunted Nixon as "Sir Richard the Chicken-Hearted" for refusing to debate him. Nixon scoffed at Humphrey as "an adult delinquent . . . the fastest, loosest tongue in the West."

In his bid to be president, Nixon used Madison Avenue ad experts to sell a "new Nixon" to the public, to erase his old "Tricky Dickie" image. "There certainly is a new Nixon," he stated at a carefully staged TV group interview. ". . . As a man gets older he learns something."

Jim Sage, a member of Nixon's TV staff, revealed confidentially, "We're moving into a period where a man is going to be merchandised on television more and more. . . . When [the public is] fed this pap about Nixon they think they're getting their money's worth. . . . Nixon has not only developed the use of the platitude, he's raised it to an art form. It appeals to the lowest common denominator of American taste. It's a farce. . . ."

Yet the public not only elected Richard Nixon in 1968 but also re-elected him in 1972. Then, with something like horror, Americans watched the Watergate scandal unfold. Nixon's resignation to escape impeachment for covering up his administration's felonies made millions of voters cynical about government.

In the 1980 contest between Democratic President Jimmy Carter and Republican challenger Ronald Reagan, Reagan scored heavily with voters by coming off the clear winner in a series of TV debates with Carter. He went to the White House.

Three years later a fresh scandal erupted when it was revealed that before those debates, the Republicans had illegally obtained secret Carter campaign materials. These tipped off Democratic strategy, enabling candidate Reagan to know beforehand exactly what Carter would say in the debates and to prepare effective answers. Top Reagan aides nervously contradicted one another in explaining their roles in having handled the pilfered materials. Seeing the parallel to Watergate, the

Martin Van Buren, depicted here in an 1848 cartoon, was careful not to take any stand in his political speeches. LITHOGRAPH BY N. CURRIER, 1848.

Ronald Reagan went to the White House in 1980 after besting incumbent Democrat Jimmy Carter. This campaign cartoon portrays what was, for Carter, a disastrous election. The elephant is the traditional symbol of the Republican party; Carter is a former peanut farmer.

media dubbed the new scandal "Debategate." Both the FBI and a House committee mounted investigations.

Another political controversy in 1983 involved a seventeen-hour TV "telethon" by Democrats to solicit contributions for their 1984 campaign, through entertainment and appeals by TV and film stars. Democrats were outraged and threatened to sue when the Republican National Committee sent cablegrams to its members urging the phoning of toll-free numbers set up by the Democrats to "tell them what you think of their unfair attacks on our party." Democratic National Committee Chairman Charles Manatt accused the Republicans of trying to tie up the phone lines so that Democratic viewers seeking to pledge campaign contributions would be discouraged by constant busy signals.

Most political campaigns have traditionally begun on the Labor Day weekend in September, with candidates addressing outings, picnics, organization conventions, or other large gatherings. Each candidate is usually backed up by a campaign manager, a staff of paid aides, and as many volunteers as the campaign is able to muster.

Campaign slogans are tested in local areas for their effectiveness; those that prove popular are proliferated in banners, buttons, bumper stickers, and media ads. In 1968 when Nixon Republicans wanted to turn the Democrats out of office, they used the slogan: "Had Enough?" Then in their campaign for Nixon's reelection, they urged: "Four More Years!"

Public-opinion surveys are used to determine the electorate's views on certain issues. Computers break down voters' views according to election districts. These statistics are evaluated to determine the views a candidate should espouse to win the largest vote.

This leads a candidate to reflect the views of constituents democratically. But it also tends to make a candidate a follower instead of a leader. As Professor Art Pearl noted, "We determine by 'scientific' means what people want, and we package our candidate accordingly."

Leonard Hall, former Republican National Committee chairman, admitted, "You sell your candidates and your programs the way a business sells its products."

Polls showing how the public is leaning toward one candidate or another are often criticized as harmful. By spotlighting a leader, they may create a "bandwagon effect"—influencing undecided voters to back a winner. They also make it more difficult for trailing candidates to raise contributions.

Critics also question poll accuracy. In 1936 a poll by a leading magazine, the *Literary Digest*, predicted a landslide victory by Alf Landon over Franklin D. Roosevelt. When instead every state but two voted for FDR, the chagrined *Literary Digest* was laughed out of business.

Aware that the public does not identify with wealthy candidates, rich men running for office do all they can to play down their economic status, while rivals emphasize it. Mississippi Senator Theodore Bilbo once accused his rival of having taken up the "upper-class" game of golf: "Golf! An effete and effeminate game that is the snare of the devil, an insult to Mississippi!"

The dirty campaign tricks in the 1972 Nixon campaign led Congress and many states to pass new laws requiring that campaign literature must reveal the identity of its sponsors as well as that of the candidate on whose behalf it is circulated. These laws now make it riskier to circulate last-minute anonymous false allegations, such as Nixon used in 1962 in his campaign to replace California Governor Pat Brown.

Two weeks before election day, the Nixon team conducted a phony poll of voters on behalf of the "Committee for the Preservation of the Democratic Party in California." Almost a million registered Democrats received mailings branding Brown a left-wing radical. A faked photo showed him with his arm around communist longshoreman-leader Harry Bridges.

Donations solicited to "bring the Democratic Party back to the middle of the road" went into the treasury of Nixon's Republican team. Governor Brown sued Nixon for issuing scurrilous and fraudulent mailings and won.

Campaigning today is an exhausting affair, with candidates for both state and national offices expected to "barnstorm" as many communities as possible in a single day. Campaign managers try to plan trips so that a candidate can dash into one town after another to shake hands in factories, on the street, and at social clubs, then dash off quickly to the next town or community. Political belief has it that every voter whose hand a candidate has clasped is a probable vote won.

To plant photos in the press and shots on TV, a candidate's advance man may urge him to cooperate in any kind of stunt from riding a mule at a picnic to going up a girder at a skyscraper under construction.

In modern campaigning, it is considered more important for a candidate to appear on TV as often as possible than to "press the flesh" in person. Just one TV appearance can often reach a thousand times more people than a candidate could with a month of personal appearances. Local and network reruns of news events increase this coverage even further.

An incumbent president seeking a second term has a great advantage over rivals within his party for the nomination. He usually has his party's political machinery at his disposal and can also use the power and trappings of his office to appear before the electorate as often as he wishes. Sometimes his renomination is such a foregone conclusion that the party worries a lack of suspense will keep bored TV viewers from tuning in to the party convention.

A sitting president can also use his office to woo the votes of disaffected minorities opposed to him by actions designed to soften their opposition. Thus in 1983 when the NAACP attacked the Reagan administration as hostile to blacks, Reagan quickly announced he was seeking new powers to enforce fair housing laws, and the Reagan Justice Department announced its first school desegregation suit, against Alabama's colleges.

Racism and prejudice still play a part in election campaigns. This truth became painfully apparent in the 1983 Chicago mayoral race between Democratic black candidate Harold Washington and his Republican opponent, Bernard Epton. Epton's campaign managers used as their campaign song lyrics set to the tune of "Bye Bye Blackbird." Epton supporters wore T-shirts emblazoned "Vote Right, Vote White." Epton slogans warned significantly: "Epton—Before It's Too Late."

Many Democratic ward bosses and voters bolted to campaign for the Republican candidate. "I've been in this business a long time," said Democratic ward committeeman John Geocaris, "and I know people vote along racial and ethnic lines. So what's wrong with that?"

When a white crowd shouted racial epithets at Washington outside St. Pascal's Roman Catholic Church, a parish priest admitted sadly, "We cannot deny that there is prejudice."

The racial issue stirred Chicago blacks to turn out at the polls in record numbers. Together with enough white Democrats who deplored the racist attacks on Washington, they managed to elect him Chicago's first black mayor. Impressed with what a solid black vote could accomplish, black leaders began talking about uniting black voters nationally behind a black presidential candidate.

In view of all the hot air dispensed on the campaign trail, it might seem that campaigning causes more confusion about candidates than it clears up. If it doesn't, it's because a good deal of cold turkey is also talked by candidates. Our country could undoubtedly use fewer politicians and more statesmen. But as a nineteenth century Maine congressman, Thomas Brackett Reed, once observed, "A statesman is a successful politician who is dead."

12

THE MAN WHO CLOWNED
HIS WAY TO THE STATE CAPITOL
—A TRUE STORY

"My fur-riends!" bawled the tubby little man on the spotlit platform. "When yew elect me—John F. Dore—the next mayor of our gre-e-at city of Seattle, yew will get a mayor who knows how to eee-conomize on city contracts. The taxpayers' money will not be used for guh-raft or coh-ruption!"

There was a sudden loud, razzing noise behind him. Dore glared around furiously. The other candidate on the platform, innocent-eyed Vic Meyers, was blowing his nose. It was one thing to suspect, but another to prove, that Meyers had a rubber razzer beneath his handkerchief. The audience guffawed.

Red faced, Dore finished his speech abruptly and sat down in a rage. Then Vic Meyers came forward into the spotlight. He blinked blandly at the still-tittering audience.

"Ladies and gentlemen," he began, pointing a melodramatic finger heavenward, "when you elect *me* mayor of Seattle, there's not gonna be any more cheap chiseling on city contracts. You know why?" He paused for emphasis, staring around solemnly. Then he added dryly, "Because I'm gonna take all the loot *myself*—and no cheap chiselers are gonna be cut in!"

The roar of laughter almost swept away John F. Dore's hopes of

142

election. He felt helpless to cope with the most unorthodox political candidate who ever burlesqued an election.

Certainly the funniest and most astonishing story in American politics is the amazing career of Victor Aloysius Meyers, five times lieutenant governor of the state of Washington and once its secretary of state.

That career began in 1932, when a group of Seattle reporters were gloomily discussing the dullness of the mayoralty campaign. There were nine candidates—mostly political hacks—seeking the voters' favor. The reporters were resigned to the election of Dore, an ultra-conservative lawyer who had the backing of most of Seattle's businessmen.

"How boring can a campaign get?" one reporter sighed. "The voters are snoring. Things are so bad that I even heard Vic Meyers wants to get into the act and jazz things up."

The reporters grinned. Everybody in Seattle knew Meyers—the screwball thirty-four-year-old bandleader who would do anything for a laugh or a headline. Once when he fell off a stepladder and broke his arm, and the story made page one, he phoned reporters to hold up their afternoon editions while he climbed back on the ladder to fracture his skull.

A loud bell rang in the mind of Doug Welch of the *Seattle Times*. Racing back to his paper, he told his editor, "Hey, I've got an idea. What if we gave a hotfoot to all those stuffy jerks running for mayor by backing a candidate who'd campaign for laughs? He'd make crazy promises with a straight face. The town would get the best laugh it's had in years. And we'd make voters realize what a bunch of incompetent windbags they keep electing to office!"

The editor grunted thoughtfully. "Who would we run?"

"Vic Meyers. Who else?"

The editor phoned the Club Victor. "Vic? I hear you're thinking of filing for mayor. If you'll go down to city hall and do it right now, I'll give you a top line in the last edition. You won't get another break like it. What do you say?"

Startled, Vic Meyers quickly assented. He was an owlish-looking, stocky man with rimless spectacles and a sparse mustache. His sense of humor had been developed as a matter of self-preservation; he was the youngest of 16 children.

Vic's musical talents were evident at an early age. By the time he was 25 he was leading his own orchestra. He quickly discovered, however, that it was his love of the ridiculous, rather than his brand of jazz, that won him space in the press. He obliged by being as nutty as a fruitcake.

Borrowing $75 from his cornet player, he raced over to the county building to file officially as a candidate. He told reporters, "I figure I better toss my hat in the ring because these other clowns are such ridiculous candidates that they're making me look like a straight man!"

The *Bellingham Herald* observed, "You may think that Seattle's leading troubador is making a laughingstock of himself with his entry into politics. Maybe he is in one sense, but don't forget that this same boy Vic is dumb—just like a fox. He never did and never will receive any less expensive publicity than this he is buying for a paltry $75 filing fee."

Commented the *Bremerton News Searchlight*: "Seattle has had injected into its coming city primary elections a bit of comedy that threatens to steal the thunder from a host of serious-minded gentlemen who are flooding the city with promises of less this and more that. Suave Vic Meyers, the orchestra leader with the elegant mustachio, has filed for the office of mayor, basing his campaign on a promise to 'jazz' things up a bit. To the outsider it's extremely laughable, but we'll bet a wooden nickel that right now some of the optimistic political leaders are wondering how many votes the baton-wielding Victor will poll."

Vic won headlines with his first campaign promise—to make Seattle a tourist mecca by serenading all incoming passengers on transcontinental trains with a jazz band. "I'll get tourists flocking in if I have to dress our traffic cops in hula skirts," he promised solemnly. "Elect me and I'll get publicity for the old town—just as I'm doing now!"

Every day saw a new campaign promise by the syncopated candidate. He intended to choose a new captain of police by his ability to play the piccolo. Daylight savings would be abolished because, as Vic explained, "I don't believe in it. Seattle should have two-four time, allegro."

Vic campaigned on a beer wagon pulled by four horses, preceded by his band playing "Happy Days Are Here Again." At busy street corners, he would make wild speeches burlesquing his rivals' campaign promises. Once a wheel of the wagon came off, precipitating Vic—accompanied by two beer kegs—into the street.

"Drink is my downfall!" yelled Vic. "*Vive le downfall!*"

One of his rivals accused, "Meyers is just a mushroom politician—a flash in the pan!"

"I resent that implication!" Vic roared. "I'm not a politician at all. But it's nice to know I've got the bums worried!"

Vic's next move stunned his opponents. He announced that Laura La Plante, a top screen star of the day, was flying up from Hollywood to become his campaign manager.

"True to my promise to inject a little color into the campaign," he declared, "I'm bringing a blond into the controversy. I've got the women's vote already. But what I need is more of the men's vote, and Laura will get it for me."

Sure enough, the stunning blond—an old friend of Vic's—flew in at Boeing Field, where he serenaded her with his jazz band. Appearing at all Vic's rallies, she attracted record crowds.

Prohibition was still the law of the land. Members of the Olympic Breakfast Club chuckled when Vic, addressing their meeting, suggested that as mayor he hoped to raise city revenues by opening a small saloon. Reading this, B. N. Hicks, state superintendent of the Anti-Saloon League, declared that he respected Meyers' lack of hypocrisy so much that he was supporting the bandleader's candidacy.

Vic threw his next bombshell at a Shrine Club luncheon. All the candidates were present, scheduled to speak. Vic waited until they were all seated. Then he shuffled in dressed as Mohandas Gandhi, leading a goat on a chain. Taking his seat at the speakers' table, he sipped goat's milk and munched raw carrots. As his dumbstruck opponents floundered through their speeches, Vic peered at them benignly over the tops of gold-rimmed "granny" spectacles.

It was the kiss of death. Vic, sitting in his bedsheet, listening with an idiotic smile, made every speech completely ridiculous. When it was his turn to speak, he grinned toothlessly—his teeth had been blacked out—and handed a card to the toastmaster. It read, "This is my day of silence."

The press agreed with the guffawing guests that Vic's rivals had been hopelessly outclassed.

At first Vic campaigned in shirt sleeves ". . . to prove there's nothing up my sleeve, and that I'm not a stuffed shirt." Then he switched to appearing in tuxedo, silk scarf, velvet-lapeled overcoat, and kid gloves. Indicating his rivals in business suits, he would shake his head sadly and explain, "Somebody's got to give this campaign a little class."

When leading contender John Dore promised government economies, Vic declared, "I'm not very thrifty myself, but you ought to see my wife! As soon as I'm elected, I'll turn the city over to her to run." He promised to put flower boxes all around the city's fire hydrants. "That," he explained, "would utilize any water that dripped out." He also planned to string hammocks at street corners, for the comfort of visiting rustics while counting the stories in Seattle's tall buildings.

Vic had a solution for getting the city's decrepit streetcar line out of the red. "We'll put beautiful hostesses on all the cars," he explained blandly. "And we'll employ professional wrestlers to open the windows. It wouldn't hurt, either, if we served certain unmentionable liquids poured over cracked ice."

Describing himself as the nation's first "maybe" candidate, he explained that candidates who said "yes" or "no" on any issue were bound to lose 50 percent of the vote. When any heckler in a crowd tried to pin him down on where he stood on a question, Vic would roll his eyes thoughtfully and then assure his listeners, "Oh, I'm okay on *that!*"

Nothing was too nutty for the unconventional candidate. He went out to an Indian reservation and beat out his platform on tom-toms. Told the Indians didn't have a vote, he declared, "Well, if they elect me, they'll get it!" He went after votes at a lumber camp by wooing the jacks with his saxophone.

Commented the *Tacoma News Tribune,* "Personal platforms are usually verbose and high-sounding, but resolve themselves down to the simple formula of 'I want the job.' Small wonder then that Seattle turns with joy and delight from the worries of a bankrupt municipal street railway to welcome the picturesque primary campaign of Vic Meyers." But some papers attacked Vic's campaign as a "sinister plot of the power trust" to distract public interest while the treasury was looted.

Candidates for political office, as the sign above this diner indicates, can come from a variety of backgrounds. Wendell Willkie, who ran for president in 1940, was once a dishwasher; Vic Meyers was a jazz musician. PHOTO BY JOHN VACHON.

Vic Meyers as Washington's lieutenant governor, February 22, 1946. WASHINGTON STATE LIBRARY PHOTO.

Despite their name, few political "cartoons" are intended to be humorous, as evidenced by this 1848 cartoon. Vic Meyers, on the other hand, found that humor was the key to his popularity. LITHOGRAPH, 1848.

Vic's use of jazz in the campaign led the president of the Chamber of Commerce, I. F. Dix, to comment dryly, "Campaign keynoters often cry for harmony. Now we can try it to music." And a former Superior Court judge, Charles Moriarty, told reporters, "Poland had a pianist—Paderewski—as premier. Why couldn't Seattle have a jazz bandleader for mayor?"

This kind of support made the zany candidate begin to wonder if he might not actually have a real chance to turn a pure farce into a political triumph. A week or so before election, Vic suddenly announced that the comedy was over. From now on he was campaigning for votes, not laughs. Refusing to wear the Gandhi costume, he began dressing in a sober business suit. Eschewing gags, he started talking about real issues.

It was a mistake. Bored, voters gave their attention to the other candidates. When the votes were counted, Vic finished sixth in a field of ten. Vic went back to his dance band at the Club Victor. But not for long. Bitten by the political bug, he decided to run for state office. Broke as usual, he was relieved to find that for only $12 he could file for lieutenant governor.

"I can't spell it," he told the clerk, "but I'll take it."

He stumped the state, tootling his saxophone and making weird campaign promises. This time his nuttiness swept him into office with a cool 40,000 majority. A reporter told him he'd have to learn parliamentary law in order to preside over the State Senate. "Phooey on that!" Vic snorted. "We're going to have nothing but good old *American* law!"

He added blandly, "I also hope that somebody tells me how to do whatever a lieutenant governor does." Somebody apparently did, because Vic was reelected four times, twice as the only Democrat surviving a Republican landslide.

As lieutenant governor, Vic horrified the political bosses by pushing bills to sweeten life for the unemployed, the aged, and dependent children. He was supported by the Washington Commonwealth Federation, a radical group.

"Just let the governor leave the state for one day," its secretary, Howard Costigan, vowed, "and Vic will show him how a state *ought* to be run!" One governor was so alarmed at this prospect that he actually didn't dare leave the state once during his entire four years in office.

He explained plaintively, "Meyers might call a special session of the legislature to listen to him play the saxophone, or to vote $100 bonuses for street cleaners." He added reflectively, "I don't know which would be worse."

Vic nevertheless managed to get enacted a lot of legislation helping the underprivileged. When Jim Farley, F.D.R.'s Postmaster General, visited Seattle, he reported in consternation, "There are forty-seven states and the Soviet of Washington!"

Political enemies tried to pin a Red label on Vic. "Who the dickens ever heard of a communist," Vic snorted, "with a middle name of Aloysius?"

He was asked how he felt about serving five consecutive terms in the state's number two spot without getting a chance at the top position. He said wistfully, "I guess with me waiting to move up, all of those governors just never dared to die!"

Vic's enemies finally unseated him in the 1952 landslide for Eisenhower. At liberty for the first time since 1932, he described himself as the best-dressed politician in the breadline.

In 1956 he campaigned for the post of Washington's secretary of state. Voters knew he was still the same old Vic when he was asked why he was a Democrat. He explained, "I don't say that all Republicans are sourpusses, but I never knew a sourpuss who wasn't a Republican!" As he once more unleashed his zany sense of humor, guffaws trailed him up and down the state.

He had sound advice for his fellow campaigners. "Spread your business out," he told them. "Make a lotta stops. Buy a quart of oil here, a gallon of gas there. You know, I once made eighteen stops en route from Seattle to Everett for a political rally. You'd be surprised at the number of votes I picked up at ten cents a glass. I never drank so much Coke in my life!"

The voters happily put Vic back in public office.

The secret of Vic Meyers' oddball political success was simple. He'd just figured out that there were more belly-laughers than sourpusses in the sovereign state of Washington.

13

SHOULD YOU VOTE
FOR THE CANDIDATE
—OR THE PARTY?

In 1960 the Republicans and Democrats agreed to have their presidential candidates confront each other in a series of TV debates. After one round between Kennedy and Nixon, a Chicago woman was asked by a reporter which candidate had persuaded her to vote for his party.

"I'm voting for Kennedy," she replied. Asked why, she explained, "Because of Nixon's eyes. Especially the left eye. Something about his eyes bothers me!"

Marshal McLuhan, authority on TV's impact on audiences, observed, "Without TV, Nixon had it made."

Some Americans vote for candidates principally because of their stand on crucial issues. Others vote largely because of party affiliation. Still others vote because of personality.

A great many voters identify with one political party or the other, often because "everybody in my family has always voted that way." Some vote for a party because it represents the value they believe in. Most Republicans tend to be conservative, high status or middle-class. Most Democrats tend to be liberal, low-income or lower middle-class. Many acquire their party loyalty even before reaching voter age.

Americans unclear about the issues in a political campaign usually play safe and vote the ticket they most trust. Since registered Democrats outnumber registered Republicans three to two, a straight party vote could almost always elect Democratic nominees, however unworthy. Fortunately Democrats refuse to give their party that power, often voting with Independents according to their own judgment of each candidate.

This is the value of a multi-party system. In any country that legalizes only one party, voters are denied a choice. The result is dictatorship instead of democracy.

Many great leaders in our history, however, did not value political parties very highly. George Washington opposed forming them, declaring in 1796, "The spirit of party . . . agitates the community with ill-founded jealousies and false alarms; kindles the animosity of one party against another; foments occasional riot and insurrection."

John Adams agreed in 1808: "Neither party will ever be able to pursue the true interest, honor, and dignity of the nation. I lament the narrow, selfish spirit of the leaders of both parties. . . . They are incorrigible."

But a twentieth century president, Republican Warren Harding, declared in 1923, "I believe in political parties. These were the essential agencies of the popular government that made us what we are. We were never perfect, but under our party system we wrought a development under representative democracy unmatched in all proclaimed liberty."

Lyndon B. Johnson, a staunch Democrat, nevertheless reminded votes of a higher loyalty. "All of us are Americans," he said, "before we are members of any political organization."

More and more Americans today are moving away from rigid party loyalty. A Michigan study made during the 1970's found that only 24 percent of that state's voters considered themselves Republicans and only 42 percent called themselves Democrats. Among voters under 30 it was found that Independents outnumbered both parties together. These findings dramatized the change since a 1958 survey found that 74 percent of voters had voted for the same party their parents had.

The new independent trend has resulted in much split-ticket voting for a presidential team on one ticket and congressmen on both tickets. This is how in 1980 voters elected Republican Reagan president, yet voted for a Democratic House.

Because TV now projects candidates into the nation's living rooms, voters can rely less and less on party affiliations and more on their own perceptions of how the candidates look and what they say. Candidate image clearly matters today far more than party image.

The print media are equally influenced. Doris A. Graber's 1972 study of 20 papers covering the 1968 Humphrey-Nixon race found that almost all reportage of the candidates' presidential qualities dealt with their personality traits, rather than with their abilities or beliefs.

The sparkling personalities of candidates like Adlai Stevenson and John F. Kennedy attracted lots of new young people into the Democratic Party. Likewise, the TV images presented by such attractive political candidates as John Lindsay, Charles Percy, Mark Hatfield, and Howard Baker brought many new enthusiasts into the Republican Party.

By the 1980's many voters seemed to have grown more politically sophisticated, more knowledgeable about the issues. Split-ticket voting was especially common among voters dedicated to special causes—for or against equal rights for women, nuclear weapons, abortion, cleaning up the environment, etc. Millions cast their ballots for candidates who had promised to advance their own passionate interests.

The most important elections in our history, in fact, have been those in which voters' choices of the issues clearly turned the country in a new direction.

When voters elected Jefferson over Adams, they opted for weaker government control of the economy and for limiting federal powers. When they voted for Polk over Clay in 1844, they approved of U.S. territorial expansion. When they made Lincoln president, they did so in opposition to slavery. When they chose Roosevelt over Hoover in 1932, they wanted the Depression ended by government intervention. And when they elected Reagan over Carter in 1980, they agreed with his program to slash federal taxes and spending to "get the government off our backs."

Sometimes a candidate who seizes on an issue becomes a "one-issue candidate" as a way of standing out from rivals and winning media attention. California Senator Alan Cranston did this in his drive for the 1984 Democratic presidential nomination by embracing the nuclear-freeze issue as his own. He won headlines but risked alienating those millions of voters who were opposed to the nuclear freeze.

Many candidates have wooed the anti-communist vote, calling for a tough stand against the Russians. "They will outbid each other in escalating the arms budget and applying a discredited policy around the world," observed Pulitzer Prize winner Robert Lasch, retired editor of the respected *St. Louis Post Dispatch.* "We should demand something more of our leaders. . . . It is long past time that we began . . . leaving it to the people of every country to pursue their own destiny, socialist or otherwise."

Sometimes when a candidate has the courage to take an unpopular stand on a controversial issue, voters respect his integrity enough to vote for him anyhow. That was the case in the 1970's when Ed Koch was running an uphill race to become mayor of New York. Talking to an audience of homeowners who favored a multi-billion-dollar highway project that he opposed, Koch told them, "I am not going to change my mind about it. If it means the difference between getting your vote and losing your vote, then I am not going to get your vote." One man rose to declare he would vote for Koch anyway, primarily because Koch didn't just tell them what they wanted to hear. Koch was elected.

Civil rights have been, and still are, a key issue in American elections. Black voters are determined to enforce those rights by electing black candidates. In 223 cities that have large black populations, there are now black mayors, 17 of them governing cities with populations of over 100,000. The number of black voters has increased by 4 million in the South alone since federal enforcement of voter registration.

"I can remember back in 1968 when Andy Young and I were arrested in Atlanta for lying down in front of some garbage trucks during a strike," recalled Rev. Joseph Lowery, president of the Southern Christian Leadership Conference (SCLC) in the early 1980's. "Today Andy is the mayor and in charge of the garbage trucks."

There are now also 21 black congressmen, over 340 black state legislators, and some 5,000 black local officials. Usually they have won those offices on the Democratic ticket.

Many whites vote for black candidates, either because they agree with the justice of increasing black political power to give them proportionate representation or because they simply agree with the candidates' views. Thus in Missouri, black state legislator Alan Wheat won a congressional seat in a district that was over 75 percent white.

Similarly, blacks will vote for a white candidate, even one running

Whether a voter chooses to cast his or her ballot for the party, or the candidate, this machine won't be used. It's a ballot box from the late nineteenth century.

When Lincoln was elected in 1860, the nation had made the decision to oppose slavery. Voters' choices of issues often decide elections. HALFTONE REPRODUCTION OF DRAWING.

CURIOUS ART OF MAKING CAMPAIGN BANNERS.

AN IMPORTANT INDUSTRY THAT SPRINGS INTO LIFE ONLY ONCE IN FOUR YEARS.

Photographs by our staff photographer, T. C. Muller. See opposite page.

Today, television brings candidates into the voter's home, but prior to that, campaigning was conducted via less direct means. This series of 1904 photos shows the process of making campaign banners. REPRODUCTION OF PAGE FROM *LESLIE'S WEEKLY*, 1904.

against a black candidate, if they favor his or her stand on the issues. Thus black votes were crucial in electing liberal white Congressman Wyche Fowler Jr. of Georgia over his conservative black opponent.

While issues are emerging increasingly as more important to American voters than party labels, voters are still strongly influenced by a candidate's image. If they are irked by their party's nomination of a candidate they dislike, they are apt to stay home on election day or vote for the opposition.

14

HOW LOBBYISTS
INFLUENCE ELECTIONS

Railroad barons in the late nineteenth century, who were major sources of campaign funds, exerted tremendous influence over American elections. Candidates they opposed were seldom elected to either state or national office.

James Bryce, an English barrister visiting the United States in 1881, was awed by the railroad lobby. "They have power," he wrote, "more power than perhaps anyone in political life except the president and the speaker, who after all hold theirs only for four years and two years, while the railroad monarch may keep his for life. When the master of one of the greatest Western lines travels toward the Pacific on his palace car, his journey is like a royal progress. Governors of states bow before him; legislatures receive him in solemn session."

Powerful lobbies are still with us today, seeking favors or legislation to benefit their special interests. They pressure legislators who are indebted to them for large campaign contributions and hope to retain their support for reelection.

There is nothing intrinsically evil in lobbying. The right of any group to "petition the government for a redress of grievances" is guaranteed by the First Amendment. But the Bill of Rights never intended the redress of grievances to be influenced by whether or not legislators received campaign contributions from petitioners.

"About 95 percent of campaign funds at the congressional level are derived from business," observed Senator Russell Long, chairman of the Senate Finance Committee. He pointed out that legislators helped their supporters get juicy government contracts, voted to cripple government agencies that regulated industries, blocked agencies seeking to enforce environmental protection laws, and voted to give government subsidies to special interests.

After being in charge of House military budgets for twenty years, Congressman Clarence Long of Maryland accused powerful corporate lobbies of controlling American foreign policy under any administration through campaign contributions. Arms and aid programs adopted by Congress, he charged, were designed to protect corporate investments overseas.

Similar concern was expressed in President Eisenhower's farewell address in 1961, when he voiced his fear that the pressure of lobbies greedy for munitions contracts and fat profits, plus the power of the Pentagon, could stampede Congress into militarizing the nation dangerously. "The potential for the disastrous rise of misplaced power exists," he warned, "and will persist."

Over twenty years later, syndicated columnist Jack Anderson pointed out, "It is doubtful that even Ike foresaw the extent to which the sweetheart relationship between Big Business and the brass has taken control of the single biggest slice of the federal government's budget pie."

In 1979 *The New York Times* reported that in the previous fall's congressional elections, special interests had contributed almost $1 million to the campaigns of just eight congressional leaders. Few realists expected those congressmen to vote against any bills the lobbies wanted passed.

Corporate lobbies exercise even greater power in state legislatures, where they can push their bills through much more easily and cheaply. State legislatures tend to meet infrequently and briefly, because salaries paid are generally so low that the legislators must maintain businesses or careers during their terms in office. Often, in their haste to adjourn, they rush through bills by voice vote—bills they have scarcely read, let alone studied. Many of these bills are written for legislators by the lobbyists.

Philadelphia reporter Bernard McCormick once noted that in the Pennsylvania legislature, the lobbyist for Sun Oil was "often referred to as the fifty-first senator," and the lobbyist for Penn Central Railroad was "considered the fifty-second."

"I have no hesitation in stating my deep conviction," declared Senator Joseph S. Clark of Pennsylvania, "that the legislatures of America . . . are presently the greatest menace to . . . the successful operation of the democatic process."

In 1983 California Secretary of State March Fong Eu warned that if the legislature didn't act to control "the unbelievable spending that is turning elections into auctions," she would introduce a citizens' initiative to control campaign spending. She pointed out that an incredible $150 million had been spent on the state's 1982 elections.

Mark Twain once observed sardonically, "I think I can say, and say with pride, that we have legislatures that bring higher prices than any in the world."

A Ford Foundation study also found that some governors accepted payoffs disguised as campaign contributions from business lobbies, in return for state contracts awarded without competitive bidding. Baltimore contractors testified that they had made such payoffs to Spiro Agnew, when he was governor of Maryland and when he was vice-president. Convicted of tax evasion, he was fined, then forced by Nixon to resign.

As early as 1852, congressional lobbies were a cause for concern. James Buchanan wrote to President Franklin Pierce, who had beaten him for the Democratic nomination, "The host of contractors, speculators, stock-jobbers, and lobby members which haunt the halls of Congress, all desirous . . . on any and every pretext to get their arms into the public treasury are sufficient to alarm every friend of his country."

Three years later a congressional investigation found that lobbyist Samuel Colt, inventor of the Colt .45 pistol, had paid a congressman $10,000 to get him a patent extension and had sought the favors of other congressmen by providing them with food, liquor, and women.

In 1873 Wisconsin Chief Justice Edward Ryan warned, "Money as a political influence is essentially corrupt . . . dangerous to the free and just administration of the law. . . . Who shall fill public stations—educated and patriotic free men, or the feudal serfs of corporate capital?"

The National Association of Manufacturers (NAM) lobby pulled its strings in 1902 to defeat labor bills for an eight-hour workday and a ban on strike injunctions. Congressmen who refused to oblige the lobby were defeated in the 1904 elections by heavy NAM contributions to their rivals' campaigns.

When Theodore Roosevelt sought reelection that year, he received large campaign contributions from the Navy League, made up of munitions makers and industrialists with Navy contracts, as well as from multimillionaires like J. P. Morgan, John D. Rockefeller, and Jay Gould. All were well repaid when Roosevelt revised the Monroe Doctrine to proclaim the right of U.S. armed forces to invade any Latin-American country failing to meet its financial obligations to foreign (U.S.) banks and wealthy investors.

A group of investigative reporters whom Roosevelt derisively labeled "muckrakers" exposed the connection between corporate lobbies and the politicians they controlled. Lincoln Steffens declared, "Our political leaders . . . conduct the government of the city, state, and nation, not for the common good, but for the special interests of private business."

Often legislators who were voted out of office were rewarded by the lobbies they had served by being hired, in turn, as lobbyists. They were expected to capitalize on their former associations to influence ex-colleagues.

Thus in 1934 the electric light and power lobby was headed by two former senators. An investigation led by Montana Senator Thomas J. Walsh characterized it as "the most formidable lobby ever brought together . . . representing capital to the amount of nearly ten billion dollars." He predicted wryly that no action would follow his committee's investigation of the lobby's corrupt practices "because it will dry up the sources of campaign funds for the next election."

In 1951 the Kefauver Senate Crime Committee hearings revealed that three men had met in a Florida hotel room to put up $150,000 each as a campaign fund for Fuller Warren's race to be governor. Apart from this half million, Warren received only $15,000 in public contributions. Soon after his election, the partner of one of Warren's three backers wrote a bill that Warren steered through the Florida legislature, freeing the billion-dollar citrus industry from all state taxes.

Look magazine reported in 1960 that lobbyists had scattered a quarter of a million dollars around the Louisiana legislature to assure passage of a right-to-work (anti-union) bill.

The Watergate scandal during the Nixon administration was, in part, about illegal campaign finances. Contributions to Nixon's Committee to Reelect the President (CRP) had been "washed" through a series of banks to conceal their sources.

Big-business lobbies, however, are not the only ones that influence elections. In 1924 organized labor provided large campaign funds that helped elect many congressmen. The new Congress passed the Railway Labor Act, giving labor more latitude in strikes. Similarly, labor's support of Franklin D. Roosevelt's campaigns was rewarded by passage of the Wagner Labor Relations Act, compelling collective bargaining.

In 1943 the Congress of Industrial Organizations (CIO) formed a political action committee (PAC) to mobilize the CIO's 5 million members in electing pro-labor candidates. When the CIO merged with the American Federation of Labor (AFL) in 1955, they organized the Committee on Public Education (COPE), which today is labor's lobby for political action.

Many other lobbies pursue what is called "single-issue politics." The Right to Life (anti-abortion) forces, for example, were responsible for defeating Iowa Democratic Senator Dick Clark's 1978 bid for reelection. Lobbies like Jerry Falwell's Moral Majority, Inc., were active in seeking to defeat congressmen who opposed prayer in the schools or who favored the Equal Rights Amendment.

Crediting lobbying by the Moral Majority for the election of Ronald Reagan in 1980, Falwell proudly asserted that "Christian people came out of the pews into the polls and caused this avalanche."

Single-issue lobbies who came to Washington empty-handed have not always received a cordial welcome. In 1894 when a severe depression led Jacob Coxey to organize a national coalition of the unemployed, Coxey's Army, to march on Washington to demand jobs, Congress

The powerful lobbies that exist today are a far cry from this 1930's parade in New York City, in which children marched for better housing conditions. AN INTERNATIONAL NEWS PHOTO.

Theodore Roosevelt, here with Admiral Evans aboard the Mayflower, repaid the Navy League for its large campaign contributions in 1904 by revising the Monroe Doctrine to increase the rights of U.S. armed forces. PHOTO BY WILLIAM H. RAN, COPYRIGHT 1908.

turned a deaf ear. Coxey and his lobbyists were jailed for walking on the grass.

And in 1970, when half a million Americans went to Washington to lobby against the Vietnam War, Nixon's Attorney General, John Mitchell, ordered mass arrests that totalled 13,400 people.

Lobbying efforts by Common Cause in the 1970's and 1980's claimed to have as their objective "returning the government to the people." This organization exposed big corporations with defense contracts that paid off helpful politicians with big campaign contributions. It also exposed how much money candidates were collecting, and from whom. Some senators and congressmen were shown to have received donations from contributors who had business before committees on which they sat in judgment.

Angry business lobbyists pointed out that the Common Cause lobby itself had spent over $442,000 in the 1982 off-year elections, almost 25 percent more than any other registered lobby. Its president, Fred Wertheimer, replied, "Many of the organizations that spend substantially more money than we do don't report at all." Other lobbies, he said, used loopholes in the disclosure law to conceal expenditures.

Some lobbies that reported spending over $100,000 each on the 1982 campaign included Handgun Control Inc., the American Petroleum Institute, the Sierra Club, the American Postal Workers Union, the American Medical Association, the Citizens Committee for the Right to Keep and Bear Arms, the U.S. League of Savings Associations, the AFL-CIO, the American Farm Bureau Federation, and the National Rifle Association (which also gave $85,000 to members of the Senate Judiciary Committee the year before it approved a bill making it easier to buy and sell firearms).

Some lobbies contribute campaign funds to both major candidates in an election, so that no matter which one wins, the lobbies are guaranteed the ear of the winner.

The political action committees, or PACs, were set up by lobbies to get around laws setting limits on a candidate's contributions from single sources. The PACs spend funds on behalf of favored candidates, ostensibly without the knowledge or control of those candidates' official campaigns. The use of PACs allows lobbies to put ten or more times the money behind a candidate than the law would allow them to contribute to his own campaign fund. During the 1981–82 election period, some 2,000 PACs contributed up to $90 million to congressional campaigns. Corporate and trade association PACs ("big business") contributed over twice as much as labor PACs (unions). PAC spending on federal campaigns was expected to reach half a billion dollars by 1992.

One of the most powerful union PACs is the National Education Association, whose teachers won from President Carter the creation of a Federal Department of Education. In 1982 its PAC spent nearly $1.5 million to back 334 candidates in the mid-term elections and helped elect 250 of them

In 1983 Republican Party leaders appealed for a removal of federal limits on political party expenditures for candidates. "Surveys repeatedly show that the public is overwhelmingly opposed to taxpayers' financing of elections," declared Nevada Senator Paul Laxalt, Republican Party chairman.

The change would lessen the influence of PACs, said Indiana Senator Richard Lugar, chairman of the Senate Republican Campaign Committee, and strengthen the role of the parties. Democrats objected because the Republicans, with access to much wealthier private financing, would benefit most.

The Democrats, meanwhile, went to a federal court to try to block conservative PACs from spending tens of millions of dollars to reelect President Reagan in 1984.

In 1983 three of the six declared candidates for the Democratic Party's presidential nomination—former Vice-President Walter Mondale, Colorado Senator Gary Hart, and Florida Governor Reubin Askew—declared they wanted no PAC support. "A president who owes his election to narrow interests," Hart explained, "risks an administration that is owned by them."

It is unquestionably true that lobbies can, through campaign contributions, affect the outcome of elections. And to the extent that they can claim credit for a candidate's victory, they can influence his decisions while in office.

The problem may never be solved until the amount of money that can be spent on election campaigns is strictly curbed by law. This change would probably require a rigid shortening of the campaign period to reduce expenses; a ban on private contributions or PACs; public funding of candidates; and apportioned free TV time for political speeches and debates.

Such reforms might mean the saving of vast millions in unnecessary expenses, fairer opportunities for all candidates, and more honest representative government for all of us.

15

STEALING VOTES

In a special Georgia election held shortly after World War II to replace deceased Governor Eugene Talmadge, his son Herman was elected. *Presumably* elected, that is. It turned out that 32 votes for him were cast by the same man under 32 different names. Only 10 of 48 write-in votes for him were legitimate; at least two voters were dead men; five had moved away; five said they hadn't voted; and another dozen voters couldn't be found. The *Atlanta Journal* won a Pulitzer Prize for exposing Herman Talmadge's stolen election.

There are many ways to steal votes. Some candidates' supporters have done it by outright fraud; some by frightening opposition voters away from the polls; some by using technicalities to disenfranchise the opposition; some by rigging election results.

Stealing votes has a long and dishonorable tradition. Colonial parties in America used mobs to terrorize opposition voters away from the polls. One of the first election riots occurred in 1742 in the Pennsylvania colony, when Scotch-Irish frontiersmen making up the Proprietary Party sought to disenfranchise Quakers. They organized a mob of 70 sailors, arming them with clubs that they "flourished over their heads with loud huzzas, and in a furious and tumultuous manner approached the place of election."

The polls were on a courthouse balcony, to which voters mounted from a street staircase. Rushing the staircase, the mob clubbed and drove off all Quakers seeking to vote. But the ordinarily non-violent Quakers quickly organized their own mob. Throwing the sailors off the staircase, they locked up 50. The election then proceeded peacefully, with a Quaker victory.

Federalist President John Adams feared the votes of French and Irish immigrants who favored Jefferson over him. So he passed the Alien and Sedition Acts to prevent aliens from becoming citizens for 14 years. Anyone daring to criticize this theft of votes was thrown in jail. Becoming president, Jefferson instantly made the Acts dead letters, so that it was easier for aliens to become citizens and vote.

In the first half of the nineteenth century, as Democrats succeeded in organizing the immigrant vote in the big cities, members of the Know-Nothing Party intensified their efforts to keep foreign-born voters from the polls. The immigrants fought back. Killings on election day were commonplace during the 1840's and 1850's.

In 1855, Know-Nothing mobs in Louisville, Kentucky, took control of the polls, beating, shooting, and stabbing Irish and German immigrants seeking to vote. When some Irish killed several rioters, enraged mobs invaded their neighborhoods, burning buildings and shooting down fleeing tenants. Twenty people died. Know-Nothing candidates swept the elections, with almost no Irish or German votes recorded.

In New York City from 1860 to 1871, police looked the other way when Boss Tweed's gangs of Tammany toughs invaded election precincts to frighten off or beat up opposition voters. Tweed also bought and bribed votes and rigged elections, until the Tammany machine was finally overthrown.

During that same period down South, it was the Ku Klux Klan that stole elections. In 1868 a congressional investigation found that in the three weeks prior to election day, 2,000 blacks had been murdered, wounded, or flogged in Louisiana. The message to blacks was loud and clear.

In the late nineteenth century, organizations proliferated whose aim was to stop "undesirables" from voting. These included the Immigration Restriction League in the East; the American Protective Association in the Midwest and Far West; the Klan and similar organizations in the

South. They sought to drive away from the polls not only immigrants and blacks, but also Catholics, Jews, Mexican-Americans, and Chinese.

In some cities, political bosses stole elections by outright fraud. Shortly after the turn of the century, muckraker Lincoln Steffens reported that St. Louis boss Edward R. Butler would walk out of a polling place and call across a cordon of police to men lounging at the curb, "Are there any more repeaters out here that want to vote again?"

Fraud was even more blatant among Philadelphians. Steffens reported that they had "no more rights at the polls than the Negroes down South. . . . The machine controls the whole process of voting, and practices fraud at every stage. The assessor's list is the voting list, and the assessor is the machine's man." A Municipal League report revealed 250 votes cast in a ward with less than 100 registered voters, the list padded with the names of dead and imaginary persons.

In one Philadelphia election, some 80,000 out of 204,000 votes were found to be fraudulent. Police had enabled repeaters to vote "without intimidation," arresting only voters who dared to protest. With the machine's own officials counting the ballots, there was no way its candidates could lose.

During the Prohibition era in Chicago, Al Capone and other gangsters contributed $300,000 to the reelection of Republican Mayor William Hale Thompson in 1927. On election day two Democratic precinct clubs were bombed, two election judges kidnapped and beaten, and voters driven from the polls by gangsters opening fire. Other voters prudently stayed home as police squads cruised the city with machine guns and tear gas. There were very few votes against Mayor Thompson.

In 1948 stealing votes was routine in Louisiana's Plaquemine Parish, bossed by Leander Perez. When Russell Long won election to the Senate that year, he freely admitted receiving several thousand votes stolen for him by Perez. When Perez introduced a law letting him plunder the local treasury, the parish's 3,000-odd registered voters wre credited with 5,361 votes in favor and 3 votes against.

During U.S. Senate Judiciary Committee hearings on why so few blacks were registered to vote in his parish, Perez explained that some white Louisiana voters charged $10 for their votes, and others charged $5, while blacks and poor whites could be bribed for only $2. "People of low character," he said, "are a little cheaper. . . . The $5 and $10 voters would not ride in the same automobile with the $2 voters when they are being brought to the polls. It was beneath their dignity."

The astonished investigator asked, "You segregated the voters according to how much you paid them?"

"Yes, sir," replied Perez blandly. He denounced any federal intervention to protect the rights of black voters as both "un-American" and "communistic."

"That," snapped Republican Senator Everett Dirksen, "is as stupid a statement as has ever been uttered in this hearing!"

Stealing elections in the old South was routine until the Civil Rights Act of 1957 established a Federal Civil Rights Commission to investigate complaints and report to the president and congress. Before then, even in communities where blacks far outnumbered whites, white officials won almost all public offices by the simple expedient of barring black voters through poll taxes that they could not afford and through hard literacy tests that only blacks were compelled to take.

Literacy tests were also used in California to exclude Hispanic citizens who didn't speak English. Ironically, the original U.S.-Mexican treaty required all California laws and proceedings to be in both Spanish and English, with the rights of Spanish-speaking citizens respected. The law that kept them from voting was passed "to protect the purity of the ballot box from the corrupting influences of the disturbing elements that come from abroad." The California Supreme Court finally set this law aside as unconstitutional in 1970.

One of the oldest and most skillful methods of stealing votes is called "gerrymandering." It was named after a signer of the Declaration of Independence, Massachusetts Governor Elbridge Gerry, who redistricted his state in 1812 in such a way that his party could win more seats in the legislature with far fewer voters than the opposition needed.

Gerrymandering works this way: Voting-district boundary lines are redrawn so that, say, a district of 40,000 largely Republican voters can elect only one representative, while another district carved out of only

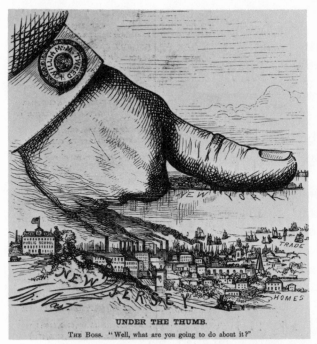

UNDER THE THUMB.

THE BOSS. "Well, what are you going to do about it?"

From 1860 to 1871, Boss Tweed bought and bribed voters in New York and New Jersey, putting voters "under his thumb." WOOD ENGRAVING AFTER THOMAS NAST IN *HARPER'S WEEKLY*, JUNE 10, 1871.

Fraud was blatant in Philadelphia, Pennsylvania elections in the late 1800's and early 1900's. In one election, some 80,000 of 204,000 votes were fraudulent. Voting lists were sometimes supplemented by the names of dead or nonexistent men. WOOD ENGRAVING FROM SKETCHES BY BERGHAUS IN *FRANK LESLIE'S ILLUSTRATED NEWSPAPER*, 1872.

The voter in this 1837 cartoon could well have been a 1948 voter, for that was when Louisiana Plaquemine Parish boss Leander Perez went so far as to segregate bribed voters by how much he had paid them. The range was from two dollars to ten dollars. LITHOGRAPH BY N. SARONY.

This cartoon shows the 1871 arrest of Boss Tweed, with the ghostly figure of an avenging Justice standing over him. WOOD ENGRAVING AFTER THOMAS NAST IN *HARPER'S WEEKLY*, 1871.

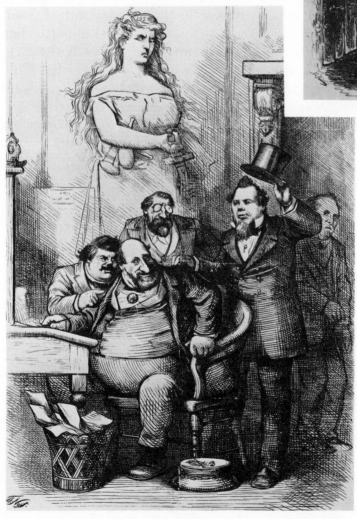

3,000 largely Democratic voters is given one representative also. In effect, the voting power of 37,000 voters has been stolen.

When Gerry re-carved voting districts for this purpose, the boundaries of one had so curious a shape that a legislator suggested it resembled a salamander. "No," replied one wit dryly, "a Gerrymander." The name stuck to the political trick.

In the late 1950's a group of blacks charged Alabama with gerrymandering the election district of Tuskegee from a square shape "into a strangely irregular 28-sided figure," which had the effect of "fencing Negro citizens out of Tuskegee."

The Supreme Court rejected Alabama's claim that it had the right to shape its political subdivisions as it saw fit. No state legislature, said Justice Felix Frankfurter in 1960, could isolate "a racial minority for special discriminatory treatment." Three years later, Justice William O. Douglas upheld the right of the federal government to rule on the fairness of districting. "The conception of political equality . . . can mean only one thing—one person, one vote," he declared. Otherwise, he pointed out, a resident of Georgia's smallest county would have 99 times the political power and influence of a citizen of Atlanta.

All state legislatures were finally forced to undertake reapportionment on a one-person, one-vote basis. District boundaries were redrawn to equalize the number of people in each election district, regardless of geographical size.

Politicians still sought to carve election districts in such a way as to tip the balance of power in them as far as possible in favor of one or the other party. In 1983 Republican George Deukmejian of California threw Democrats into an uproar by announcing a special election to try to redistrict the state so that the Republicans could win the legislature.

No other group of Americans was rendered as powerless through having their votes stolen as Southern blacks, even as late as the 1960's. After the passage of civil rights acts, when Northern sympathizers went South to aid in black voter-registration drives, many were terrorized and beaten. Some were murdered.

Fannie Lou Hamer, a black militant, reported in 1964, "I tried to register in 1962. I was fired the same day, after working on the planta-

Elbridge Gerry, looking rather satisfied in this portrait, redistricted his state of Massachusetts in 1812 so that his party would win more seats in the legislature. Gerrymandering is one of the most effective ways of stealing elections, but no state can get away with it today. ENGRAVING BY J. B. LONGACRE FROM A DRAWING BY VANDERLYN.

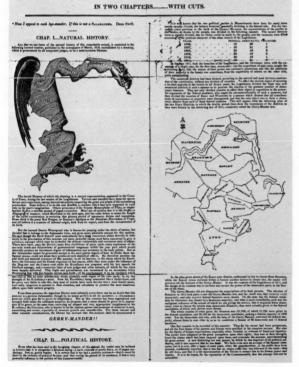

When a legislator suggested in 1812 that the boundaries of one newly founded district resembled a salamander, someone else dubbed it a "Gerrymander." Gerrymandering became the subject of political cartoons such as this. BROADSIDE, 1815.

President Lyndon Johnson signed the Voting Rights Act in 1965, which suspended literacy tests used to bar blacks from the polls.

tion for eighteen years. . . . When my employer found out I'd been down to the courthouse, she said I'd have to withdraw or be fired. 'We are not ready for this in Mississippi,' she said. 'Well, I wasn't registering for you,' I told her, 'I was trying to register for myself.'"

One voter-registration drive was mounted in 80 percent black Lowndes County, Alabama, in the spring of 1965, because out of 15,000 resident blacks, not a single one had been allowed to register.

The Voting Rights Act of 1965 suspended literacy tests and other means used to bar blacks from the polls. Federal examiners were appointed for all voting districts where less than half the population was registered to vote. Anyone trying to stop a citizen from registering or voting was made subject to arrest on criminal charges. Shortly afterward the Supreme Court ruled all poll taxes unconstitutional.

The effect of the Voting Rights Act in Mississippi was impressive. Before its passage, only 35,000 blacks had been registered in the whole state; after passage, the number jumped to 200,000. By November, 1967, they were able to elect 22 blacks to public office in the state.

Even so, black votes were still being stolen by 1983, when black leader Rev. Jesse Jackson challenged William Reynolds, chief of the Justice Department's Civil Rights Division, to join him in rural Mississippi for a firsthand look at voting rights abuses. Reynolds discovered registration offices that closed at county officials' whims; employers who refused to let blacks leave work to register; polling places moved from black to white neighborhoods without notice; black voters turned away by white imposters posing as federal officials.

"I never heard of anything like that before," Reynolds admitted. He dispatched federal examiners to five Mississippi counties to stop such abuses and register black voters.

Today, because of changes in the law and stricter enforcement, elections are generally more honest, for the most part, than they were in darker periods of our history. There will always be some vote stealing here and there, just as there is some dishonesty in law, medicine, business, or any other facet of American life. But the vast majority of us can count on voting, and on our vote counting—unless we rob ourselves of our vote by failing to go to the polls.

16

"WHAT DIFFERENCE
DOES MY VOTE MAKE?"

Ever hear of President Charles Evans Hughes?

You would have, if just one more voter in each California district had voted for him, sending him to the White House instead of letting Woodrow Wilson remain in it in 1916.

Many Americans don't bother exercising their franchise, feeling that the vote of one more person isn't going to make any difference in the results of an election. Some explain that they're too busy or have more important things to do. Others shrug and say that they're simply not interested in politics.

In 1964 a public-opinion poll found that three out of four Americans trusted the government to do what was right most of the time. But another poll in 1978 found only 28 percent expressing such trust, with 65 percent by then convinced that the government was run on behalf of a few big interests.

One might have expected such disillusionment to result in a widespread determination to "vote the rascals out." Instead, 65 percent expressed the belief that ordinary people had little to say about what the government does. Their apathy was reflected by a sharp decline in registration and voting.

Yet even presidential races have often been so close that they were decided by the few extra votes of citizens who cared enough to cast their ballots. In 1884 Grover Cleveland was elected over James G. Blaine when, out of over a million New Yorkers who voted, just 1,149 more chose Cleveland.

And in 1960 John F. Kennedy was sent to the White House instead of Richard Nixon by an average of less than a single vote per election precinct.

Even world history could have been changed by a single vote. That was the margin by which Adolf Hitler was elected leader of the Nazis in a 1932 party election. Had he lost by a single vote instead, there might have been no World War II.

Sometimes minorities feel discouraged from voting because they are always outnumbered. Then something happens that lets them discover their strength when anger drives them to vote.

After the Civil War, President Andrew Johnson sought to pacify white Southerners by weakening the Civil Rights Act. In 1868 angry blacks went to the polls in record numbers to vote against him. The black vote proved decisive in sending Ulysses S. Grant to the White House.

Since 1872, there have been eight presidents who went to the White House with less than a majority of the popular vote—Hayes, Garfield, Cleveland, Harrison, Wilson, Truman, Kennedy, and Nixon. The significance of this is that had the small number of third-party votes gone to their opponents instead, those eight presidents would not have been elected. The importance of even a handful of votes cannot be overestimated.

While your vote may or may not be crucial in an election, casting it gives you the healthy satisfaction of acting out your convictions. "Always vote for a principle, though you vote alone," advised John Quincy Adams, "and you may cherish the sweet reflection that your vote is never lost."

Some citizens who ignore the polls on election day feel that it doesn't matter because plenty of others will be voting. If everyone felt the same way, of course, there would be no elections and, in a little while, no more democracy.

"The whole system of American government rests on the ballot box,"

President Calvin Coolidge declared in 1926. "Unless citizens do their duties there, such a system of government is doomed to failure."

One might expect young Americans who pass their eighteenth birthdays to rush enthusiastically to the ballot box in an election year to exercise their right to choose the leaders they want. Ironically, records show that young people 18 through 25 have the poorest voting turnout of any age group. A 1974 Census study found only about 40 percent registered to vote.

This lack of participation disturbed presidential candidate Hubert Humphrey, who resented criticism of American politics by youths who failed to vote. "If you think politics is a little dirty," he challenged them, "why don't you get a bar of Ivory soap and get in and clean it up instead of sitting out there in the bleachers?"

At a 1980 rally of Reagan supporters, Paul Weyrich, director of the Committee for the Survival of a Free Congress, admitted frankly, "I don't want everyone to vote. Our leverage in the election quite candidly goes up as the voting populace goes down. We have no responsibility, moral or otherwise, to turn out our opposition. It's important to turn out those who are with us."

If you have the vote and fail to use it, you may allow a candidate you oppose to slip into office by a slim margin. Then, despite barely escaping defeat, he may claim that his election represents a "mandate from the people" to put into effect the very laws you fear and oppose, ignoring the fact he was elected by only a minority of registered voters.

One of the most valuable services any young American can perform, whether of voting age or below, is to help get out the vote, making certain that as many eligible voters as possible register and express their choices at the polls. The larger the turnout, the more the results will represent the true will of the majority. The smaller the turnout, the easier it is for pressure groups to steamroller an election.

"A registration and get-out-the-vote drive is hard work," admitted John Bailey, a past chairman of the Democratic National Committee. "There is little glamour in it. But it is the most essential of all political activity. It is what puts the votes in the ballot box on election day."

There is a wide choice of volunteer jobs awaiting those willing to join in getting out the vote. Needed are checkers to work at the polls and

What difference can one vote make? In 1932, Adolf Hitler was elected leader of the Nazi party by only one vote. In a less spectacular but nevertheless close election, Grover Cleveland was elected president in 1884. PHOTO COPYRIGHT APRIL 1, 1908.

Like Cleveland, President John F. Kennedy was elected to the office by less than a majority of the popular vote. Other presidents with this distinction: Hayes, Garfield, Harrison, Wilson, Truman, and Nixon.

note registered voters who haven't shown up; messengers to convey this information; telephoners to contact the absentees; drivers to take voters to the polls; and baby-sitters to take care of youngsters while their parents vote.

When racist opposition was intense in the South during the early 1960's, many idealistic Northern youths volunteered to go South in buses to help get out the black vote. They persisted in the drive even when some were shot, beaten, gassed, whipped, and jailed. One youth, his arm in a sling after being beaten by a police baton, told a reporter, "If blacks can't register to vote, then what's all this democracy we hear so much about?" Since that drive, the number of black voters in the South has jumped to over 4 million.

More and more American blacks up North, too, were realizing that the answer to many of their problems lay in getting a better deal from their local, state, and federal governments. And the only way to do that was to get out the black vote to support candidates who would work toward that goal.

When black Harold Washington ran for mayor of Chicago in 1983, his campaign attracted a huge black voter turnout. Among black youths 18 to 25, only 10 percent of whom normally voted, fully 90 percent flocked to the polls. Washington's election thrilled and inspired blacks everywhere.

As a direct result, over 100 black young volunteers showed up in Boston to organize voter-registration drives for the 1984 presidential election, even though this was 19 months off.

"It's unheard of," marvelled black City Councilor Bruce Bolling. "Generally people don't think about registration until two months before the election."

Other ethnic groups like Mexican-Americans and Cuban-Americans were impressed. They began cooperating with blacks to support candidates pledged to help minorities. All political parties began paying more attention to the minority vote.

"In the final analysis, it is up to you," Patrick J. McGarvey, a former CIA agent, reminded American voters. "It is the boom of your voice that will bring about the necessary changes. As an individual you no doubt have a feeling of impotence when it comes to influencing your government. Collectively, however, you have tremendous impact. It requires only that you get a slight ground swell started."

Turning out the vote is one way to do that. Any citizen of any age with a burning desire to stop injustice and a willingness to get others to sign on is a one-person dynamo.

"What old people say you cannot do, you try and find that you can," Thoreau advised youth in *Walden*. "Old deeds for old people, and new deeds for new."

Thomas Carlyle reminded us, "Every new opinion, at its starting, is precisely in a minority of one." And as Henrik Ibsen pointed out, the majority of today was the minority of twenty years ago, because it takes that long for progressive ideas to prevail and transform popular opinion.

If you want to participate in getting out the vote, you can join 120,000 Teen Age Republicans in any of 50 states, or the Young Democrats of America in over 40 states. The American Student Association has branches in many colleges. COPE, the AFL-CIO's political-action arm, recruits young volunteers. The League of Women Voters is a non-partisan organization devoted to working for open and responsive government. The National Organization for Women (NOW) works for policies that will bring women into the mainstream of American society. And there are many third parties that would eagerly welcome the aid of as many young volunteers as they can get.

Check your local phone book for the names and phone numbers of the organization you'd like to work with. If it isn't listed, phone the local office of your state or federal representative for this information.

It's your country. If you care about it, use your vote when you have it, and help your fellow citizens use theirs.

Or would you rather turn the country over to political bosses to run it as they please?

17

IS YOUR JOB DONE
WHEN YOUR CANDIDATE WINS?

In 1964, while the Vietnam civil war raged, Americans voted for Lyndon Johnson as president because of his promise of a "Great Society" program, which would end poverty in America, and his assurances about Vietnam: "We don't want our American boys to do the fighting for Asian boys. We don't want to get . . . tied down in a land war in Asia."

Yet Johnson let his Great Society program go by default, throwing America's resources instead into sending half a million American boys to fight the most unpopular war in our history. His broken promises outraged millions of Democrats who had voted for him. They flooded the White House with tons of protesting mail and staged huge anti-war demonstrations.

Johnson did not dare to run for another term.

As when your favorite baseball, football, or basketball team wins the season's honors, it's highly satisfying when your favorite candidates or political party wins an election. But the consequences are vastly more important. One week after a sports team is victorious, the event is ancient history and has no further impact on your life. But for the length of an election term, the victorious candidates or party will affect your life by the laws they pass.

If you have voted for or helped get out the vote for the winning side, you may feel that your job is done. Your choices are in place, and now it's up to them to do all the things they promised during the campaign. It's okay now to sit back and "let George do it." Right?

Wrong. Often much of what has been promised during a campaign turns out to be empty oratory. Elected officials or the party may give halfhearted lip service to the goals they promised to the electorate, but then they take no real action to achieve them through legislation. Or they may enact a watered-down, weak, ineffective law that is really a betrayal of their pledge.

Moreover, as new problems arise, a candidate you elected may take a position in dealing with them that you strongly oppose. Just because you've elected leaders to represent you, does that mean you're obligated to support everything they do? Those in office are responsible to the people who elected them. They need to hear from their constituents when their decisions are disappointing, especially in issues of such life-and-death importance as peace and war.

A case in point was the decision of President James Polk to declare war on Mexico in 1846 in order to seize huge areas of Mexican land. Far from docilely accepting this decision, the voters of every New England state reprimanded him sharply. The Massachusetts legislature even flirted with charges of treason by resolving that it was the patriotic duty of "all good citizens to join in efforts to arrest this war."

Similarly, in 1916 Woodrow Wilson campaigned on the slogan, "He kept us out of the war." And just one year earlier he had promised, "We will not ask our young men to spend the best years of their lives making soldiers of themselves!"

Then in 1917 Wilson reversed himself and took the country into World War I. There was deep bitterness among those who had voted for him to keep America at peace, and many dared to speak out openly against the war. Hundreds, including Eugene Debs, were imprisoned under a new Sedition Act rushed through Congress to make "disloyal language" a felony.

No group of Americans is better qualified to testify as to the broken promises of government officials than native Americans. Despite dozens of treaties signed with native American tribes, the government has broken almost every one, seizing their best lands and driving them onto arid reservations.

Government officials turned a deaf ear to their complaints until finally Senator Robert Kennedy headed a new subcommittee to investigate conditions on the reservations. "I am doing my best," he told a group of native American students in one state, "to get you your civil rights."

"Never mind our civil rights, Senator," one young man replied wryly. "Just get us back our country!"

Voters weary of being deceived about Vietnam under the Johnson administration listened to Republican candidate Richard Nixon promise, "It's time we once again had an open administration—open to the ideas from the people and open in its communication with the people— an administration of open doors, open eyes, and open minds." He also promised voters an administration dedicated to "law and order."

Voters elected him in 1968, only to get an administration that proved one of the most dishonest and lawless administrations in the history of the country—the administration that expanded the Vietnam War for four more years and that ended in the Watergate scandal.

But as Nixon himself noted in his book *Six Crises*, "Voters quickly forget what a man says." He proved it by winning a second term despite his broken promises, largely because the full extent of his criminal behavior had not yet been exposed by election day of 1972. When it was, however, public outrage was so great that an avalanche of angry mail forced even Republican congressmen to announce they would vote for his impeachment.

The media serve America well when they remind voters of the discrepancy between what politicians say and what they do. This makes it more difficult for them to shift positions when it is politically expedient. When California Senator Alan Cranston announced his candidacy for the 1984 Democratic presidential nomination, he sought to unite all the nuclear-freeze forces behind him. He declared himself "convinced that, in the long run, we cannot revive our economy—or save our society— until we end the incredibly dangerous, shamefully expensive arms race." That won much liberal support.

But the media pointed out that Cranston had supported President

Reagan's decision to revive the costly B-1 bomber, which would be built in Cranston's home state. Was expediency, the media asked, more important than principle?

Australian correspondent Elisabeth Wynhausen, stationed in Washington, found discrepancies between President Reagan's claims and his performance. Checking on his claim that as governor of California he had reduced the public payroll, she found that during his governorship, the number of state public servants had increased by 21 percent instead.

Campaigning for president, he had promised a balanced budget by 1984. Elected, he declared that it was unrealistic not to expect a national deficit of $100 billion at least. He had campaigned with promises to weed out "waste, fraud, and mismanagement." Elected, he had demanded record billions for the Pentagon, which all government agencies agreed was the worst culprit in waste, fraud, and mismanagement. Campaigning, he had attacked arms control negotiations with the Soviet Union as "appeasement." Elected, he promised to speed up arms control talks with the Russians.

Widespread public protest forced Reagan to backtrack on some of his initiatives. When he violated the 1980 Republican platform plank opposing the withholding of a percentage of interest and dividends for the Internal Revenue Service, a deluge of protest mail caused Congress to delay his proposal indefinitely.

Even *Reader's Digest*, an enthusiastic Reagan supporter, criticized him for his appointees to head the Environmental Protection Agency (EPA), whom he praised as well qualified to provide the nation with clear air and water. The *Digest* revealed that, by secret agreement with White House officials, the agency's assignment to clean up dangerous dumps and spills was sabotaged, protecting the industries responsible.

A different Republican president, Dwight D. Eisenhower, had declared, "There may be some cynics who think that a platform is just a list of platitudes to lure the naive voter—a sort of facade behind which candidates sneak into power and then do just as they please. I am not one of these."

Most historians agreed that he was not.

It needs to be pointed out that some candidates do honestly try to keep their campaign promises when they win election. Often, however,

A vote for James Polk in 1844 was a vote for U.S. territorial expansion, but when he declared war on Mexico in 1846 so the U.S. could seize Mexican land, every New England state opposed his decision. LITHOGRAPH BY P. HAAS, 1844.

When the Narragansett Indians offered shelter to Roger Williams, little did the native Americans realize what was to follow. Despite dozens of treaties that U.S. government officials signed, the government broke almost every one and stole the Indians' land, confining them to reservations. ENGRAVING BY J. C. ARMYTAGE AFTER A. H. WRAY.

they depend heavily on campaign funds contributed by special interests that expect legislation favoring them. Such candidates have to weigh conscience against practicality. They may listen to their conscience if enough voters pressure them to vote in the public interest.

There are several ways you can try to hold elected candidates to their campaign promises, forcing them to pay attention to your disagreement with their policies. The easiest and best is to write them letters. Representatives and senators, state as well as national, are sensitive to voter reactions in their mail. So are presidents, governors, and state, county, and local officials. They also pay attention to letters to the editors of newspapers and magazines, because such letters are read and considered by thousands of voters.

Public officials pay particular attention to letters of protest from those who have helped to elect them, whether by contributions, votes, or helping in their campaigns. They hope that they can count on the same support for their reelection campaigns. Thus it becomes important for them either to change their stand or to persuade dissatisfied supporters that their stand is a correct one.

Another way to express disapproval of elected officials' behavior in office is through state primary elections. When you vote against a president, governor, senator, representative, mayor, or other elected official in a state primary, you are sending that candidate a message. The size of the official's reduced vote lets him know clearly how much he has failed to live up to his constituents' expectations.

If enough voters are disillusioned, and the official is defeated, his successor will also get the message. The chances are then brighter that this time you will get the kind of administration you voted for.

18

HOW OTHER COUNTRIES CHOOSE THEIR LEADERS

An intriguing view of early American elections through European eyes was provided in 1835 by a young Frenchman, Count Alexis de Tocqueville, when he wrote a book about his visit to America four years earlier. Tocqueville was dubious about French interest in borrowing the American practice of universal suffrage. He felt that the animosity of the masses toward the better-educated classes would result in the election of uneducated incompetents to public office.

That had already happened in America, he noted. The election of roughnecks like Andrew Jackson, Sam Houston, and Davy Crockett to public office showed "how far wrong the people can go . . . to be represented by people of their own kind." It was deplorable that a "David Crockett, who has no education, can read with difficulty, has no property, no fixed residence, but passes his life hunting," should be considered qualified to help make the nation's laws in Congress.

Tocqueville sympathized with leading Americans who refused to seek public office: "To win votes one has to descend to maneuvers that disgust distinguished men. You have to haunt the taverns and dispute with the populace: That's what they call *electioneering* in America."

He expected all New World democracies to become tyrannies through the abuse of power by their elected incompetents.

The election of President Andrew Jackson horrified French Count Alexis de Tocqueville, who wrote that it exemplified "how far wrong the people can go . . . to be represented by people of their own kind." This picture is of Jackson's inaugural reception in 1828. COLONIAL AQUA-TINT BY ROBERT CRUIKSHANK IN THE PLAYFAIR PAPERS, 1841.

"It's through this . . . evil," Tocqueville predicted darkly, "that the American republics will perish."

The secret ballot is as old as the ancient Roman Republic, where it was first adopted in 139 B.C. But the kings who ruled Europe for centuries afterward did not take kindly to any kind of ballot, secret or otherwise. Prince Clemens von Metternich, who forged the Holy Alliance of European monarchs in 1815, warned them that a growing demand for popular elections threatened their thrones.

"Rule must come from above, not below," he cautioned.

But the spread of the Industrial Revolution doomed the old order. Constitutional government gradually spread throughout Europe in the nineteenth century, even though many monarchs were allowed to remain on their thrones as figureheads.

For the first half of the century, votes had to be cast openly under the grim observation of powerful monarchist factions, who could mark opposing voters for reprisal. Finally public pressure forced France to adopt the secret ballot in 1852. Italy followed the trend in 1859. England resisted secret voting at parliamentary and municipal elections until 1872.

The twentieth century saw the rise of a new threat to the institution of free elections in Europe—dictatorship.

When the old Czarist regime in Russia was overturned by revolution in 1917, the Russian people won the right to vote for the first time in their history. But not for long. The Bolshevik Party soon seized power, substituting a "dictatorship of the proletariat" for elected public officials. Only a small band of dedicated Marxists, the communists insisted, was qualified to govern a nation for the benefit of the masses. Elections were scorned as a bourgeois system by which the ruling classes deceived and controlled the people for profit.

The next important challenge to free elections came in the Italy of King Victor Emmanuel, when Fascist leader Benito Mussolini ran for a seat in the Chamber of Deputies in 1921. His Blackshirt followers organized torchlight parades, tossed bombs into socialist meetings, and beat up opponents and forced castor oil down their throats. A year later,

Mussolini led a march on Rome, seizing power as prime minister.

"We Fascists throw poisonous ideas about liberty on the rubbish heap!" he roared in a balcony speech to a huge crowd. "Italians are tired of liberty. They want and need order, authority, discipline!" Although he scoffed at voting as a "childish game," Mussolini held fraudulent elections in 1924 to "prove" to the world that the Italian people supported his dictatorship. His Blackshirt squads broke up rival meetings, terrorized voters at the polls, stuffed the ballot boxes, then tallied the votes and announced their leader's "victory."

From then until Mussolini's downfall during World War II, the only elections held were those in which Fascists alone were permitted to run. "I prefer fifty thousand rifles to five thousand votes," Mussolini once cried. "A party in power has the duty to defend itself against all!"

Mussolini's example inspired Germany's Adolf Hitler, leader of the Nazi Party, whose Brownshirts waged street warfare against working-class and Jewish districts. By 1932 Hitler had captured over a third of the popular electoral vote and was able to compel his appointment as chancellor of Germany. He lost no time in seizing total power as dictator.

"The man who feels called upon to govern a people has no right to say, 'If you want me or summon me, I will cooperate,'" he explained. "No! It is his duty to step forward!"

That was the end of free elections in Nazi Germany.

Another dictatorship arose in Spain, when Generalissimo Francisco Franco, with military aid from Hitler and Mussolini, led a revolt against the legally elected republican (Loyalist) government in 1936. After the Fascists had shot their way to power three years later, Franco proclaimed himself *Caudillo*, Chief of State for Life. His firing squads executed 30,000 republican prisoners. He ruled Spain with an iron fist until his death in 1975, when liberal King Juan Carlos took power and subsequently restored free elections to Spain.

Portugal became a republic after the overthrow of its monarchy in 1910. But in the next sixteen years, there were 24 revolutions and 44 changes of government. Finally, in 1926 the military seized power, establishing a dictatorship under Antonio de Oliveira Salazar. When several thousand Portuguese signed a petition urging free elections,

Salazar had his secret police locate these "Red intellectuals" for "correction."

Pressured by Portugal's Western allies, Salazar announced elections for 1949. When a political opponent took him seriously and tried to run, Salazar denounced him as a public enemy, compelling him to withdraw his candidacy. The tactic was repeated in 1951. Unopposed, Salazar "won" each time.

Not until 1958 did an air force general, Humberto Delgado, dare defy Salazar by stumping the country to campaign against him. Rigging the election as usual, the dictator declared Delgado the loser. The Bishop of Oporto indignantly cried fraud. Salazar promptly went on TV to announce that he was abolishing popular elections and punishing all "agitators." Delgado, who prudently fled to Brazil, was subsequently murdered.

Illness forced Salazar's retirement in 1968. After several succeeding military dictatorships, popular discontent finally restored elections to Portugal in 1975.

For centuries most Asian people were governed by either autocratic monarchs or Western colonial powers. The first break in this pattern came in 1912, when forces led by republican Sun Yat-sen finally overthrew the Manchu dynasty in China. But his republic was quickly subverted by warlords and their ally, Chiang Kai-shek, who kept China a dictatorship.

In 1948 communist forces led by Mao Tse-tung overthrew Chiang and the warlords, only to establish a Marxist dictatorship under which free elections were still forbidden. That situation still prevails in the China of today.

In 1954, inspired by Mao, Vietnam communist leader Ho Chi Minh led Vietminh revolutionists against ruling French colonial forces and defeated them. A peace settlement at Geneva was guaranteed by the British, the Russians, the Chinese, and the Americans, who withdrew, however, while promising not to interfere with the Geneva Accords.

This agreement decreed that the French were to withdraw to the south, and Ho Chi Minh's forces to the north, to prepare for nationwide

Italian dictator Benito Mussolini held
fraudulent elections in 1924 to prove that
people supported him. His Blackshirt
squads terrorized voters and counted the
votes themselves to guarantee his victory.
Mussolini's tactics were a source of
inspiration to Adolf Hitler and his
Brownshirts. PHOTO BY UNDERWOOD &
UNDERWOOD.

Hitler and Mussolini aided Generalissimo
Francisco Franco in establishing his
dictatorship in Spain. Franco proclaimed
himself Chief of State for Life, and he had
30,000 republican prisoners executed to
seal that proclamation. He died in 1975,
after ruling Spain for almost 40 years.
PHOTO BY ALFONSO.

elections two years later that would determine a unified government for all Vietnamese.

"I have never talked or corresponded with a person knowledgeable in Indochinese affairs," President Eisenhower subsequently admitted, "who did not agree that had the elections been held as of the time of the fighting, possibly 80 percent of the population would have voted for Ho Chi Minh."

They never got the chance because Eisenhower's secretary of state, John Foster Dulles, was determined to sabotage the Geneva Accords. He set up a puppet government in South Vietnam, which rejected the scheduled elections. The result was the disastrous Vietnam War, involving an American intervention with troops that was denounced by most nations in the world.

When outraged American public opinion finally forced the Nixon administration to sign a peace that extracted U.S. forces from the Vietnamese quagmire, North Vietnam quickly overran and defeated South Vietnam. They could then have held the long-postponed national elections and probably have won. The elections were never held. As in other countries where the communists won power militarily, there were no further free elections. Elections represented a dangerous precedent for the future.

After World War II, African nations began to fight off the yoke of colonialism. The first to succeed was the Belgian Congo, now called Zaire, which won its freedom and the right to hold its first election in 1960. Almost 200 tribes speaking 400 different languages and dialects participated. Murders of each other's candidates were not uncommon. Polling booths were wrecked, election officials beaten. Rival tribes speared each other in the streets. The elections left some 60 dead, hundreds wounded.

The omens were not too bright for the peaceful transition of other former African colonies to new democracies.

Closer to home, the Cuban people had suffered under the tyrannical and corrupt rule of U.S.-supported dictator Fulgencio Batista until 1959, when he was overthrown by a popular revolution led by Fidel Castro.

Castro instituted sweeping reforms benefiting the poor Cuban masses at the expense of the middle classes, many of whom fled to the United States.

Most journalists who covered the Cuban revolution agreed that if elections had been held, Castro would have been the overwhelming choice of the people. But he resisted all demands for elections, saying, "They would be unfair because I would be swept into office."

At a May Day rally in 1961, he told a huge crowd that elections were unnecessary: "A revolution expressing the will of the people is an election every day, not every four years; it is a constant meeting with the people, like this meeting. The old politicians could never have gathered as many votes as there are people here tonight to support the revolution."

When he asked the crowd to express their will, they roared back the answer he wanted: *"No elections!"*

One bitter opponent, Urrutia Lléo, declared, "Castro's maneuver was successful. He knew that the people would reject the kind of elections that had been held so often before in Cuba, and he did not offer them better ones, democratic, honest elections."

The U.S. State Department cited Castro's refusal to hold elections as proof that Cuba was a communist state. But Castro did not turn to the Soviet Union for aid until Washington had rejected his appeal for a U.S.-Cuban accord and had instead sought to overthrow him by the Bay of Pigs invasion.

In India, Prime Minister Indira Gandhi was found guilty in 1975 of violating the election laws to win her seat in Parliament. Faced with demands for her resignation, she declared a state of emergency instead and assumed dictatorial powers. Tens of thousands of her political opponents were jailed. Censoring the press, she suspended further elections. Angry dissenters fought running gun battles with police.

Turmoil in India grew so great that Gandhi was finally forced to dissolve Parliament in 1977 and announced new elections for March. She tried to rig them against the opposition, but she failed. Voted decisively out of office, she sought to mollify the citizens by restoring civil liberties, abolishing censorship, freeing political prisoners, and then resigning. But she was imprisoned awhile for her misdeeds.

Nevertheless three years later the Indians forgave her, electing her to a second chance as prime minister. This time, she promised, India would continue to operate as a democracy.

Fresh political storms brewed in 1983 over a scheduled election in the state of Assam, where Hindus were enraged over the heavy immigration of Muslim Bengalis from Bangladesh. Boycotting the election, which the Bengalis were expected to win, the Hindus demanded that Gandhi cancel it. Perhaps because her party would gain from the Bengali vote, she refused. The result was a horrifying massacre.

Ten thousand Hindus in Assam marched with guns, spears, and arrows against 50 Muslim villages. They burned huts, chased the villagers into cornfields, and hunted them down like rabbits. Women and children were killed. As village after village burned to the ground, the death toll exceeded 3,000.

Such are the lethal passions that can swirl around foreign elections deciding supremacy between mortal enemies.

The British electoral system differs from ours in a number of significant ways. We vote for a president. The English vote for a party; the party that wins the most seats in Parliament forms a government, and its leader becomes prime minister. Our president's term is four years. Each Parliament sits for five years, but it can be dissolved by a vote of no confidence in the government or by new elections called sooner by the prime minister.

Traditionally, Britain has given its voters a choice between the Conservative Party and the Labor Party. A split in Labor's ranks, however, has produced a third-party alliance of Social Democrats and Liberals. This split allowed Conservative Prime Minister Margaret Thatcher to remain in power in a 1983 election with only 43.1 percent of the total vote.

Britain also has its share of tiny splinter parties, many of them expressing the British sense of humor at the cost of a $240 filing fee. There are the Nobody Party, the Independent Mushroom Party, the Ban the Old Fogeys Party, the Best Party I've Ever Been To Party, Freddie's Alternative Medicine Party, and Jim the Fish Conservative Independent Party.

The Official Monster Raving Looney Party ran against Thatcher in her own home constituency. Its leader, Screaming Lord Sutch, campaigned with the slogan: "Give a vote for insanity. You know it makes sense!"

Australia offers its voters a choice between the Labor Party and the conservative Liberal/Country Party. Voting is compulsory, with fines for any citizen who fails to vote in a national election. In 1983 an Australia newspaper accused the American CIA of secretly interfering in a previous election in order to defeat the Labor Party.

The French elect their president for a seven-year term. He appoints the premier. The French Parliament consists of a National Assembly and Senate. The president has the right to dissolve the Assembly and call for new elections.

There are many different French parties, no one of which holds a majority in Parliament. Most laws are passed by a coalition between parties. France turned socialist in the spring of 1981 with the election of François Mitterand as president. In municipal elections 22 months later, the dissatisfied French voted heavily anti-socialist. But like him or lump him, Mitterand would remain their president for another five years.

After World War II, a defeated Germany was divided into the Federal Republic of Germany (West Germany), a democracy allied to Europe and the U.S.; and the German Democratic Republic (East Germany), a communist state linked to the Soviet Union. More than the ugly Berlin Wall erected by East Germany divides the two German governments.

West Germany is governed by a Parliament, whose *Bundestag* members are elected for four-year terms. Together with an appointed upper chamber, the *Bundesrat*, they elect a president for a five-year term. The *Bundestag* alone chooses the chancellor, or prime minister. The major parties are the Social Democratic Party and the Christian Democratic Union/Christian Social Union Party.

Something of a stir was created in 1983 when a new party called the Greens, supported by German youth, won five seats in the *Bundestag*. They marched to Parliament wearing jeans and sweaters, in a festive parade featuring banners, bongo drums, and flowers. The Greens vowed to work against nuclear power plants, acid rain, the East-West arms race, and NATO.

West German elections have a remarkably high voluntary voter turnout. A European Community study found the levels of political discussion in West Germany to be the highest on the continent, a remarkable turnaround for a people who, under the Nazis, did not dare express a controversial opinion.

East German citizens have little to say about how they are governed. That is determined by the Socialist Unity (communist) Party, which handpicks the 500 deputies who are "elected" to the People's Chamber for five-year terms. The Chamber chooses the Council of State and Council of Ministers who carry on executive functions. But the real power in East Germany is suggested by 400,000 Soviet troops garrisoned there.

On the other hand, in communist Yugoslavia, non-communists can run for office. There is also relative freedom to criticize the government, unusual in a communist society, although advocating its overthrow could result in arrest.

Yugoslavs vote for delegates, who then vote for the councils that run the nation's six republics and the federal government. A policy of rotating the national leadership annually gives each republic's council representative a chance to be president. This system prevents any one official from becoming a dictator or any one republic from becoming dominant.

Hungary, too, is liberalizing its regime. Non-communist candidates have been permitted to run for office in 39 of the nation's 352 parliamentary districts. Under new proposals for 1985 sponsored by communist officials, up to 85 percent of seats in the National Assembly will be open to non-communists.

From 1967 to 1974 Greece was a dictatorship ruled by a military regime known as "the Colonels," who seized power. A public uproar finally compelled them to agree to elections, which brought about a socialist government. Most Greeks I spoke to during my visit there in 1983 told me that it had made little difference in their lives, except that they now felt free to say anything they pleased in the daily political discussions that go on in the *tavernas*.

Television plays a major role in many West European countries. Britain, Sweden, Denmark, Norway, the Netherlands, and West Germany give generous TV coverage to important political debates. No political advertising is permitted at election time, but free time is made available for party broadcasts.

Twelve political parties in the Dutch Parliament are given ten minutes of TV time four times a year, with extra time at elections. In Britain political broadcasts are shown on all channels, so that viewers cannot escape exposure.

No elections have been more controversial than those in Central America. In El Salvador revolutionists sought to overthrow a brutal government that used army troops and rightist "death squads" to murder dissenters and innocent villagers. Despite its persistent human rights violations, which included the murders of three American nuns and one American laywoman church worker, the government was supported by the Reagan administration.

In 1982 the junta in power, prodded by President Reagan, staged elections in El Salvador, which, however, were supervised by its brutal troops. The rebels led a boycott of the election, warning that leftists who tried to vote were likely to be seized and shot. The junta assured a large turnout by letting it be known that Salvadorans who couldn't show proof of having voted might be suspected of being rebel supporters.

The junta won the election, which the rebels disdained as unfree and unrepresentative. President Reagan sought to increase military and economic aid to El Salvador, calling it a vital ally in fighting the spread of communism in Central America. But Congress was appalled when the junta arrested 23 Salvadoran teachers for "terrorism," while the army also kidnapped scores of trade-union and political leaders. Amnesty International protested the junta's capture and torture of political prisoners.

Refusing to increase any aid to the brutal regime until there was proof it was reforming, Congress also demanded that President Reagan compel the junta to enter into negotiations with the rebels for a peaceful solution to the civil war.

What about elections in the nation that is the leading challenger of the United States for world influence?

In the Soviet Union, nomination is tantamount to election. One candidate for each local post is chosen in small, closed meetings controlled by the Communist Party, the union committee in a factory or commune, or often by both together.

Asked why two or more candidates were not nominated for a post, a Soviet official replied, "It would mean you think one of them is not good enough for the office. We don't want to insult our candidates."

Nominations for deputies to the Supreme Soviet take place at a club or Palace of Culture. Officials in the Communist Party apparatus indicate who is to be nominated. Speeches are made on behalf of the candidates. Their nomination, voted on by a show of hands, is always approved unanimously.

Candidates chosen are usually Party members who excel in their jobs and in demonstrated civic concern. Nominated because of the respect they command in their communities, they often have little knowledge of the workings of government. This is not considered important as long as they follow the Party line. Important legislation does not originate with the Supreme Soviet, which is largely a rubber stamp for decisions made by the Party's *Politburo*, the ruling body of the Soviet Union. Deputies facilitate execution of policy, not its formulation.

"The old deputies will tell me what to do," one newly elected deputy explained, "and I'll carry out my assignments."

During the last ten days of election campaigns, voters are visited by candidates and Party workers speaking in their behalf. These occasions also allow voters to voice grievances they would like the candidates to take care of.

Elections are viewed basically as a public vote of confidence in the Soviet regime. As election day draws closer, scarce food items suddenly become abundant in the stores. Soviet papers overflow with praise for communist accomplishments since the Revolution. Bookstores display brochures attacking Western bourgeois elections. These charge that monopolists manipulate and control those elections through fraud and bribery; that blacks and minorities are prevented from voting; and that candidates can be elected by a minority vote, unlike Soviet candidates, who usually get 100 percent of the vote.

On election day, polls are set up in schools, Palaces of Culture, and other public places. They are usually decorated with flowers, pictures of Lenin, and red banners with communist slogans. Sometimes there are refreshments and a brass band to reward voters. There are no voting machines. Since there is usually only one candidate for each post, voters can either mark their ballots or just drop them in an urn.

All voters have their names checked off a voting list that tells poll watchers who has failed to vote. By mid-afternoon nonvoters are contacted and reminded of their civic duty. This follow-up has different implications in the Soviet Union than in Western democracies like ours. Soviet elections have something like a 99 percent turnout because few Russians care to attract suspicion, by refusing to vote, that they are dissenters.

On the rare occasions when an angry Russian may enter a voting booth, scratch off the name of the official candidate, and write in his own choice, his vote is invalidated because his candidate has not been nominated and approved.

Soviet elections cost only a tiny fraction of what is spent on American elections. Most campaign workers are unpaid volunteers. Candidates pay nothing in campaign expenses.

The significant difference between Soviet and American elections is, of course, that Russian voters never have the option of turning out one government and installing a new one. They cannot reject and reverse a government policy they don't like. And they have no real choice of candidates to represent them. No free elections, in the Western sense, can be said to exist in the Soviet Union.

It would boggle the mind if 70 percent of American candidates elected to Congress were suddenly to be arrested and executed by the president of the United States. Yet former Premier Nikita Khrushchev revealed that in 1934 Josef Stalin had done just that to Soviet deputies: "It was determined that of the 139 members and candidates of the Party's Central Committee who were elected at the Seventeenth Congress, 98 persons, i.e., 70 percent, were arrested and shot."

Western democracies, with all their shortcomings, still offer their citizens a free choice of candidates and programs.

Dictatorships have an advantage in that their unlimited powers en-able them to act more swiftly than democracies. It only takes a change of mind by one person or a few people to change the whole course of government.

A constitutional democracy, on the other hand, is deliberately slowed down by checks and balances. Power and authority are divided among a president, Congress, and Supreme Court; or a prime minister, Parliament, and High Court.

These precautions also make it difficult for any one person or group in a democracy to gain enough power to impose a dictatorship upon its people. That is the great strength of all democratic electoral systems, including our own.

19

WHAT'S GOOD
AND WHAT'S BAD
ABOUT OUR SYSTEM

No one would claim that our electoral system is perfect.

We have had notable presidents like Thomas Jefferson, Abraham Lincoln, and Franklin D. Roosevelt. But our system has also put into the White House presidents who were "eminently forgettable" mediocrities like Millard Fillmore, Franklin Pierce, and James Buchanan; and presidents like Ulysses S. Grant, Warren Harding, and Richard M. Nixon whose administrations were corrupt.

Certainly no electoral system can guarantee that only the finest, most intelligent and honest chief executive will emerge victorious. But one has to question why Americans have so often made poor choices.

During the Nixon administration, the American public was shocked by disclosure of the Watergate scandal. They were stunned further when tapes of conversations within the White House were made public, revealing the president and his aides as cynical, vulgar, dishonest, and corrupt. After Nixon was forced to resign and many of his aides went to jail, millions wondered how they could have been so misled as to have voted for such an administration not just once, but twice.

Perhaps we need to pay less attention to political propaganda and self-serving pitches by candidates and parties, and more to factual campaign information provided by such organizations as the League of Women Voters and Common Cause.

Some voters are dissatisfied with the convention system of the two major parties because often the candidates chosen, instead of being the best each party can offer, represent a compromise between opposing factions within each party. The electorate is then faced with a choice of two unexciting major candidates. Consequently, many disgusted voters either stay home on election day or protest by voting for a third party.

During the 1960's and early 1970's, voters became disillusioned about professional politicians after Vietnam and Watergate. Democrat Jimmy Carter won election promising that his administration would stay close to the people because he was not part of the Washington Establishment. Similarly, Republican Ronald Reagan won election by promising voters to "get the federal government off our backs."

The election of presidents who lack national experience is a mistake, argues Nelson W. Polsby of the University of California at Berkeley in his book *Consequences of Party Reform*. "That our two most recent presidents [Carter and Reagan] should be arguably the two most nationally inexperienced in American history," he declares, "cuts directly across the grain of common sense that tells us that duties of the presidency are not smaller today than when more seasoned candidates . . . were routinely the only ones considered qualified for the job."

Our turnout at the polls, poor at best in the past, seems gradually to be growing even worse. In 1960 slightly over 3 in 5 citizens voted in a presidential election. This percentage steadily declined until the 1980 election, when only 53.9 percent of the population—slightly over half—bothered going to the polls. Thus Ronald Reagan was elected president by less than 28 percent of Americans eligible to vote.

Perhaps one reason is that we're too engrossed in our private affairs to pay attention to shaping the government we live under. As long ago as 1896, M. I. Ostrogorski, a Russian visitor observing American politics, reflected, "The desperate race for wealth has absorbed the citizen and has not left him time to attend to the public welfare; it even encouraged his want of public spirit and converted it almost into a virtue."

George E. Reedy, former press secretary to President Lyndon B. Johnson, thinks the problem lies in public dissatisfaction with mediocre, muddling White House leadership. Perhaps we need to shake off resignation and apathy by getting mad instead—mad enough to "turn the rascals out."

On election day, that is our time-honored form of peaceful revolution, one of the great strengths of our electoral system. As long as we enjoy the right to vote against candidates, parties, and programs we oppose, we can feel confident of living in freedom. Even if our choices are mistaken, as they often are, we will always have another opportunity to reverse them at the next regular election . . . if only we take it.

One serious defect in our electoral system is the advantage large campaign funds give to some candidates. As the law presently operates, huge sums can be spent on behalf of a candidate's campaign as long as he presumably does not have control of those expenditures himself.

Trade association, labor union, corporation, and other PACs were revealed to have spent $83 million on behalf of 1982 congressional candidates. "When PACs give money they expect something in return other than good government," observed Republican Senator Robert Dole, chairman of the Senate Finance Committee.

Democrat Representative Thomas Downey declared, "You can't buy a congressman for five thousand dollars, but you can buy his vote on a particular issue." There are 3,371 PACs of all kinds, only a quarter of them pro-labor.

"The financing of elections must be altered if there is to be authenticity in our society," insists Professor Art Pearl. "A campaign *by* Big Money must also be a campaign run *for* Big Money. That leaves us no alternative but to think small—to spend no more money than needed, to build a mass base of large numbers of persons contributing modest amounts. . . . If contribution is monopolized by the few, the quality of life must suffer for the majority."

England's campaign period is only one month. If we could shorten ours, the cost of running for election could be reduced tremendously. There would be many benefits. Candidates would have less need of PACs. Money would be less of an obstacle to running for office. Fewer voters would be bored by yearlong campaigning, and more would be willing to pay attention during the month before election day.

On the other hand, our present lengthy campaigns do serve to help educate voters. During the 1960's, for example, the clashing campaigns of Barry Goldwater and Lyndon Johnson made voters think deeply about the issues of nuclear war. The campaigns of George Wallace, Strom Thurmond, and Robert Kennedy made voters sensitive to racial

THE CRADLE OF THE G.O.P.

FIRST REPUBLICAN CONVENTION HELD AT LAFAYETTE HALL, PITTSBURG, PA, FEB, 22ᴰ 1856.

LITHOGRAPH BY ARMOR LITHOGRAPH COMPANY, 1897

GET OUT !!

G.O.P. PROTECTION

FREE TRADE DEMOCRACY

FULL DINNER PAIL

TRYING TO KICK IT OVER.

POLITICAL CARTOON BY LEON BARRITT, OCTOBER 1, 1904

Perhaps voters should turn their attention from political propaganda and self-serving campaign speeches to factual information provided by organizations such as the League of Women Voters and Common Cause.

LITHOGRAPH PRINTED BY B. THURSTON, 1856

issues. The campaigns of Hubert Humphrey, George McGovern, and Richard Nixon made them think deeply about the Vietnam War. Such campaigns serve to crystalize views of controversial problems.

Public-opinion polls are both a minus and a plus in our electoral process. Critics charge that they don't merely sample public opinion, but also create or change it. A poll may ask a loaded question that elicits answers favoring one candidate or position. Polls also create a "bandwagon effect." People like to vote with a winner, to bet on a favorite.

If polls show a candidate in the lead for either nomination or election, a certain number of voters are likely to be influenced to jump on that bandwagon. That candidate also finds it easier to win financial support from PACs, which desire to back a winner who will be obligated to them.

Polls can't, of course, be outlawed. They're part of a free press, of the people's right to know. And they do satisfy public curiosity about how well candidates are doing, who seems to be forging ahead, and which issues are prevailing. In that sense they serve the electoral process well, because they contribute to the interest in a campaign race.

Perhaps what's needed is greater public awareness that polls are only straws in the wind. Voters' minds change from week to week with new developments. Schools could also help by educating tomorrow's voters to think for themselves, rather than follow the herd just to "be with a winner."

There is controversy over the role of the media in our elections. Conservatives accuse them of being biased in favor of liberal candidates because many reporters and editors are liberals. On the other hand, liberal and radical candidates accuse the media of being under the thumb of their wealthy owners and big advertisers, slanting campaign coverage to favor conservative candidates.

Presidential candidates have often complained about the media's scrutiny, which Democratic Senator George McGovern labeled often "beyond reason." When he had delivered a major campaign address, the media had largely ignored it, playing up instead a personal feud between two of his staff members.

When a newspaper had attacked the wife of Democratic Senator Edmund Muskie in 1972, he was moved to tears of outrage in public.

The media blew up the incident as an alleged indication of instability, and Muskie's presidential candidacy was destroyed.

When Republican Governor George Romney reversed his support of the Vietnam War, explaining that he had been previously "brainwashed" by the administration's "snow job," the media ended his chances by calling him "the brainwashed candidate."

When Republican President Jerry Ford sought to be elected to a term of his own, he said, in answer to a question, that he didn't think the Polish people considered themselves dominated by the Soviet Union. His error was magnified by the media into an indictment that he was totally ignorant about foreign affairs. It helped defeat his candidacy.

Presidents complain, too, about media reportage once they are elected. But with all their faults, the American media are still free—which means free to make mistakes and free to be unfair from time to time. Would anyone trade them for controlled media that report only what the government allows?

A major flaw in our electoral system is its discrimination against women. They have a hard time unseating male officials in office, who have decided advantages as incumbents—name recognition, party support, favors done for constituents, easy access to campaign funds. They are also handicapped by the myth that women aren't qualified to be politicians.

PACs contribute to far more men than women. One reason is contacts made by men on golf links, at business lunches, at fraternal organizations, at the Chamber of Commerce, etc.—opportunities that are mostly closed to women. When women do get contributions, those are usually only a fraction of the money given to male candidates.

One of the more urgent needs for reforming our electoral system, most political experts agree, is the abolition of the Electoral College, so that citizens can vote directly for their presidential choice instead of for electors with that power.

Unless we make that change, it is quite possible that a candidate may become president even though most of us vote for his opponent. If he wins a state's popular vote by just a single ballot, he gets that state's entire electoral vote. Many similar slim wins give him a lot of electors.

Thus he may win the election with a majority of Electoral College votes, even though his opponent gets a majority of the popular vote.

Countless efforts have been made in Congress to abolish the Electoral College, but none have succeeded to date because of reluctance to tamper with our traditional electoral machinery. We can expect a fresh public uproar, however, the next time a candidate wins the White House while losing the popular vote.

The increasing practice of American voters in splitting their tickets, instead of voting for all candidates of a single party, has resulted in what some see as a weakness of our electoral system, while others regard it as a strength.

A president may be of one party, while the majority of one or both houses of Congress may be of the other. The same is true of a governor and his legislature. This can create serious problems if what a president or governor wants, the Congress or state legislature doesn't. Or vice versa. Thus there may be constant squabbles, a series of executive vetoes, and legislation piling up un-passed.

On the other hand, this division of power also provides a series of checks and balances. Neither the chief executive nor the legislators get their way entirely. Often they are compelled to compromise, so that the final legislation that emerges does not ride roughshod over the wishes of the voters who support either party.

The quality of our elections might improve if some way could be found to make voters blind to the color of a candidate's skin. Too often the campaigns of black or Hispanic candidates provoke a backlash of racism, with many voters casting ballots out of prejudice, regardless of the candidates' qualifications or the excellence of their programs.

It is understandable that such prejudice would anger blacks and Hispanics into voting as a bloc for minority candidates. But one can only hope for the day when *all* of us vote for candidates purely on the basis of their character, qualifications, and record, and what they pledge to accomplish in office.

A minor flaw in our electoral system is the time difference in reporting election results, because of the three-hour lag between closing of the polls in the East and on the West Coast. In 1980, when it became clear that Republican Ronald Reagan had won decisively over Democrat

Jimmy Carter, Carter graciously and publicly acknowledged defeat soon after early results began coming in, and while the West Coast was still voting.

California's Democratic candidates were furious. They lost votes when many of the state's Democratic voters, hearing Carter's concession on TV, didn't bother going to the polls. They demanded that, in the future, either no election results be broadcast until California voting had ended or all polls shut down at the identical moment, regardless of the different time zones. This would require a compromise as to the hours all polls would be open.

The United States has probably the most elaborate, complicated, and expensive electoral system in the world. It operates according to a kaleidoscope of national, state, and local party rules, state statutes, and special rulings by federal, state, and local courts.

Political maneuvering also goes on for much longer than in any other country. Some critics complain that no sooner is an administration elected than it prepares for the next election.

Yet, with all its shortcomings, our system is recognized as one of the best and most flexible in the world. Consider how we have been able to transfer power peacefully in the most turbulent of times, as during the Vietnam War, civil rights riots, and the Watergate crisis, instead of by violence or armed insurrection. Even when America has been at war abroad, or within itself as during the Civil War, we have continued to hold our elections on schedule. And each time, citizens have been free to vote whether to continue an administration in office or to end it.

When a dictator or junta seizes power, the people of that country have no voice in their own destiny. Even when a coup or uprising with sincerely patriotic motives overturns a tyrannical government, the longer the new dictatorship remains in power without free elections, the more it begins to resemble the tyranny it overthrew. "Power tends to corrupt," said the British historian Lord Acton; "absolute power corrupts absolutely."

That is why, in the United States, we give no presidential administration longer than four years in office without compelling it to submit to new elections. As President Wilson once said, "America is safe only because we do not know who the presidents of the United States are going to be."

In his book *Landslide*, Professor Art Pearl urges students—the voters of tomorrow—to get involved in the electoral process as early as possible. This requires, he says, that "everyone gets with some *political* organization, pays dues, and gets involved in policy determination and candidate selection. . . . *Now* is the time to be involved . . . in your community."

To participate properly in the machinery of our democracy, we need to attend political meetings and work for causes and candidates we believe in. If we don't, a handful of activists are likely to operate and control our governments—local, state, and national. We need to understand the direct link between politics and our personal benefit. If we fail to look after our own interests, why should we expect strangers with different goals to do it for us?

When there is misgovernment in Washington, state capitols, or local offices, it is easy to blame political leaders. But those leaders did not get in power without our votes. As Lincoln Steffens once observed, "The misgovernment of the American people is misgovernment *by* the American people."

We need to work inside the political parties to help select candidates of the highest integrity, instead of permitting political bosses to foist their choices on us. To keep the power out of their hands, more of us have to seek election as convention delegates.

We need to be aware, moreover, that there are among us some who would like to see elections outlawed. They are not many, but they are often tightly organized in paramilitary groups seeking to establish an American dictatorship.

For example, in California, John Capricorn heads a paramilitary group called Orion Nebula 18. "The military order will take possession of the government," he predicts. "What this country needs is a good military dictatorship . . . to straighten out people's perspective."

The only way to keep groups like this at bay is to make certain, by our participation, that the electoral system remains the only way to change our government. "The ballot," Lincoln said, "is stronger than the bullet."

Another way you can participate in the political process is through writing your local officials, state legislators, Senators, and Representatives, letting them know what you think about the issues that concern you. This is an excellent way of making your voice and your views heard, and you don't have to be of voting age. Even if a thirteen-year-old youth writes, an elected official needs to pay attention, because that youth probably has at least two adult voters in the family.

"I read every letter written me by a constituent," declared Arizona Representative Morris K. Udall. "A staff member may process it initially, but it will be answered and I will insist on reading it and personally signing the reply."

Sometimes the candidates we vote for turn out to be terrible choices. As one wit put it wryly, "I'm superstitious—I believe that voting brings four years of bad luck." But lots of other decisions we make also turn out wrong. That doesn't stop us from trying to make better decisions in the future.

And we *have* had some outstanding Americans serving us in the White House, Congress, governor's mansions, and city halls. If we learn all we can about the candidates and the issues and get involved in the electoral process, we're bound to elect a lot more fine leaders.

One of them, in fact, might eventually be *you*.

APPENDIX
Presidential Winners and Losers

DATE	WINNER	LOSER
1789	George Washington (F)	John Adams (F)
1792	George Washington (F)	John Adams (F)
1796	John Adams (F)	Thomas Jefferson (D-R)
1800	Thomas Jefferson (D-R)	Aaron Burr (D-R)
1804	Thomas Jefferson (D-R)	Charles C. Pinckney (F)
1808	James Madison (D-R)	Charles C. Pinckney (F)
1812	James Madison (D-R)	De Witt Clinton (F)
1816	James Monroe (D-R)	Rufus King (F)
1820	James Monroe (D-R)	John Quincy Adams (N-R)
1824	John Quincy Adams (N-R)	Andrew Jackson (D)
1828	Andrew Jackson (D)	John Quincy Adams (N-R)
1832	Andrew Jackson (D)	Henry Clay (N-R)
1836	Martin Van Buren (D)	William Henry Harrison (W)
1840	William Henry Harrison (W), replaced by Vice-President John Tyler (W) in 1841	Martin Van Buren (D)
1844	James K. Polk (D)	Henry Clay (W)
1848	Zachary Taylor (W), replaced by Vice-President Millard Fillmore (W) in 1850	Lewis Cass (D)
1852	Franklin Pierce (D)	Winfield Scott (W)
1856	James Buchanan (D)	John Charles Frémont (R)
1860	Abraham Lincoln (R)	Stephen A. Douglas (D)
1864	Abraham Lincoln (R), replaced by Vice-President Andrew Johnson (R) in 1865	George B. McClellan (D)
1868	Ulysses S. Grant (R)	Horatio Seymour (D)
1872	Ulysses S. Grant (R)	Horace Greeley (D/Lib. R)
1876	Rutherford B. Hayes (R)	Samuel Jones Tilden (D)
1880	James A. Garfield (R), replaced by Vice-President Chester A. Arthur (R) in 1881	Winfield Scott Hancock (D)
1884	Grover Cleveland (D)	James Gillespie Blaine (R)
1888	Benjamin Harrison (R)	Grover Cleveland (D)
1892	Grover Cleveland (D)	Benjamin Harrison (R)
1896	William McKinley (R)	William Jennings Bryan (D, Pop.)
1900	William McKinley (R), replaced by Vice-President Theodore Roosevelt (R) in 1901	William Jennings Bryan (D)

1904	Theodore Roosevelt (R)	Alton Brooks Parker (D)
1908	William H. Taft (R)	William Jennings Bryan (D)
1912	Woodrow Wilson (D)	Theodore Roosevelt (Prog.)
1916	Woodrow Wilson (D)	Charles Evans Hughes (R)
1920	Warren G. Harding (R), replaced by Vice-President Calvin Coolidge (R) in 1923	James Middleton Cox (D)
1924	Calvin Coolidge (R)	John William Davis (D)
1928	Herbert Hoover (R)	Alfred Emanuel Smith (R)
1932	Franklin D. Roosevelt (D)	Herbert Hoover (R)
1936	Franklin D. Roosevelt (D)	Alfred M. Landon (R)
1940	Franklin D. Roosevelt (D)	Wendell Willkie (R)
1944	Franklin D. Roosevelt (D), replaced by Vice-President Harry S Truman (D) in 1945	Thomas Edmund Dewey (R)
1948	Harry S Truman (D)	Thomas Edmund Dewey (R)
1952	Dwight D. Eisenhower (R)	Adlai Ewing Stevenson II (D)
1956	Dwight D. Eisenhower (R)	Adlai Ewing Stevenson II (D)
1960	John F. Kennedy (D), replaced by Vice-President Lyndon B. Johnson (D) in 1963	Richard Milhous Nixon (R)
1964	Lyndon B. Johnson (D)	Barry Morris Goldwater (R)
1968	Richard M. Nixon (R)	Hubert Horatio Humphrey, Jr. (D)
1972	Richard M. Nixon (R), replaced by Vice-President Gerald R. Ford (R) in 1974	George Stanley McGovern (D)
1976	James E. Carter (D)	Gerald R. Ford (R)
1980	Ronald Reagan (R)	James E. Carter (D)

POLITICAL PARTY LEGEND

F = Federalist	D = Democrat
D-R = Democratic-Republican	Prog. = Progressive
N-R = National-Republican	Pop. = Populist
W = Whig	Lib. R = Liberal Republican
R = Republican	

Bibliography and Recommended Reading
(*indicates recommended reading)

Archer, Jules. *Angry Abolitionist: William Lloyd Garrison.* New York: Julian Messner, 1969.

———. *Battlefield President: Dwight D. Eisenhower.* New York: Julian Messner, 1967.

———. *Colossus of Europe: Metternich.* New York: Julian Messner, 1970.

*———. *The Dictators.* New York: Hawthorn Books, Inc., Publishers, 1967.

*———. *The Extremists: Gadflies of American Society.* New York: Hawthorn Books, Inc., Publishers, 1969.

———. *Famous Young Rebels.* New York: Julian Messner, 1973.

———. *Fighting Journalist: Horace Greeley.* New York: Julian Messner, 1966.

———. *Hawks, Doves, and the Eagle.* New York: Hawthorn Books, Inc., Publishers, 1970.

———. *Ho Chi Minh: The Legend of Hanoi.* New York: Crowell-Collier Press, 1971.

———. *Indian Foe, Indian Friend.* New York: Crowell-Collier Press, 1970.

———. *Laws That Changed America.* New York: Criterion Books, 1967.

*———. *1968: Year of Crisis.* New York: Julian Messner, 1971.

*———. *The Plot to Seize the White House.* New York: Hawthorn Books, Inc., Publishers, 1973.

*———. *Police State.* New York: Harper & Row, Publishers, 1977.

*———. *Resistance.* Philadelphia: Macrae Smith Company, 1973.

*———. *Revolution In Our Time.* New York: Julian Messner, 1971.

*———. *Riot! A History of Mob Action in the United States.* New York: Hawthorn Books, Inc., Publishers, 1974.

———. *The Russians and the Americans.* New York: Hawthorn Books, Inc., Publishers, 1975.

———. *Strikes, Bombs, and Bullets: Big Bill Haywood and the I.W.W.* New York: Julian Messner, 1972.

———. *Superspies: The Secret Side of Government.* New York: Delacorte Press, 1977.

———. *Thorn In Our Flesh: Castro's Cuba.* New York: Cowles Book Company, Inc., 1970.

———. *They Made a Revolution: 1776.* New York: Scholastic Book Services, 1973. St. Martin's Press, 1975.

———. *Treason in America: Disloyalty Versus Dissent.* New York: Hawthorn Books, Inc., Publishers, 1971.

———. *Twentieth-Century Caesar: Benito Mussolini.* New York: Julian Messner, 1964.

———. *Uneasy Friendship: France and the United States.* New York: Four Winds Press, 1972.

———. *The Unpopular Ones.* New York: Crowell-Collier Press, 1968.

*———. *Washington vs. Main Street.* New York: Thomas Y. Crowell Company, 1975.

*———. *Watergate: America in Crisis.* New York: Thomas Y. Crowell Company, 1975.

*———. *Who's Running Your Life?* New York and London: Harcourt Brace Jovanovich, 1979.

*———. *World Citizen: Woodrow Wilson.* New York: Julian Messner, 1967.

Bibliography

*———. *You and the Law.* New York and London: Harcourt Brace Jovanovich, 1978.

*———. *You Can't Do That to Me!* New York and London: Macmillan Publishing Co., Inc., 1980.

*Atkins, Chester G. *Getting Elected: A Guide to Winning State and Local Office.* Boston: Houghton Mifflin Company, 1973.

Bailey, Thomas A. *Presidential Greatness.* New York: Appleton-Century, 1969.

Baker, Kendall L., Russell J. Dalton, and Kai Hildebrandt. *Germany Transformed.* Cambridge and London: Harvard University Press, 1981.

*Barber, James David, ed. *Choosing the President.* Englewood Cliffs, N.J.: Prentice Hall, Inc., 1974.

*Broder, David and staff of the *Washington Post.* *The Pursuit of the Presidency: 1980.* New York: Berkley Books, 1980.

*Bruno, Jerry and Jeff Greenfield. *The Advance Man.* New York: William Morrow and Company, Inc., 1971.

Clavir, Judy and John Spitzer, eds. *The Conspiracy Trial.* Indianapolis/New York: The Bobbs-Merrill Company, 1970.

*Deuel, Wallace R. *People Under Hitler.* New York: Harcourt Brace and Company, 1942.

*Domhoff, G. William. *Fat Cats and Democrats: The Role of the Rich in the Party of the Common Man.* Englewood Cliffs, N.J.: Prentice Hall, 1972.

*Dorman, Michael. *Under 21.* New York: Dell Publishing Co., Inc., 1970.

*Douglas, William O. *The Right of the People.* New York: Arena Books, 1972.

Durant, John and Alice. *Pictorial History of American Presidents.* New York: A. S. Barnes and Company, 1955.

*Ferguson, Thomas and Joel Rogers, eds. *The Hidden Election.* New York: Pantheon Books, 1981.

Gosnell, Harold F. and Richard Smoka. *American Parties and Elections.* Columbus, Ohio: C. E. Merrill, 1976.

Green, Timothy. *The Universal Eye.* New York: Stein and Day, Publishers, 1972.

*Greenfield, Jeff. *Playing to Win: An Insider's Guide to Politics.* New York: Simon & Schuster, 1980.

*Gregory, Dick. *Dick Gregory's Political Primer.* New York: Harper & Row, Publishers, 1972.

Haldeman, H. R. *The Ends of Power.* New York: Times Books, 1978.

Harnsberger, Caroline Thomas. *Treasury of Presidential Quotations.* Chicago: Follett Publishing Company, 1964.

*Hoopes, Roy. *Getting With Politics.* New York: Dell Publishing Company, 1968.

Johnston, Mary. *Roman Life.* Chicago: Scott Foreman and Company, 1975.

*Lebedoff, David. *Ward Number Six.* New York: Charles Scribner's Sons, 1972.

Leinwand, Gerald, ed. *Civil Rights and Civil Liberties.* New York: Washington Square Press, Inc., 1968.

Leish, Kenneth W. *The American Heritage Pictorial History of the Presidents of the United States* (3 vols.). New York: American Heritage Publishing Co., Inc., 1968.

Levy, Mark R. *The Ethnic Factor: How America's Minorities Decide Elections.* New York: Simon and Schuster, 1972.

*Mandel, Ruth B. *In the Running: The New Woman's Candidate.* New Haven and New York: Ticknor & Fields, 1981.

Bibliography

Martin, Michael and Leonard Gelber, eds. *The New Dictionary of American History*. New York: Philosophical Library, 1965.

Masters, Nicholas A. and Mary E. Baluss. *The Growing Power of the Presidency*. New York: Parents' Magazine Press, 1968.

*McGinnis, Joe. *The Selling of the President: 1968*. New York: Trident Press, 1969.

Morris, Richard B., ed. *Encyclopedia of American History*. New York: Harper & Row, Publishers, 1965.

*Mote, Max E. *Soviet Local and Republic Elections*. Stanford: Stanford University Press, 1965.

*Murphy, William T. Jr. and Edward Schneier. *Vote Power: How to Work for the Person You Want Elected*. Anchor Press, 1974.

Nash, Gerald D. *The Great Transition*. Boston: Allyn and Bacon, Inc., 1971.

*Neuborne, Burt and Arthur Eisenberg. *The Rights of Candidates and Voters*. New York: Avon Books, 1976.

*Nie, Norman H., Sidney Verba and John R. Petrocik. *The Changing American Voter*. Cambridge & Boston: Harvard University Press, 1979.

*Paizis, Suzanne. *Getting Her Elected: A Political Woman's Handbook*. Sacramento, Calif.: Creative Editions Publishing Co., 1977.

*Papele, Henry. *Banners, Buttons, and Songs: A Pictorial Review of America's Presidential Campaigns*. Cincinnati: World Library Publications, Inc., 1968.

*Pearl, Arthur. *Landslide*. Secaucus, N.J.: The Citadel Press, 1973.

*Polsby, Nelson W. and Aaron Wildavsky. *Presidential Elections: Strategies of American Electoral Politics*. New York: Charles Scribner's Sons, 1980.

Quigley, Charles N., exec. dir. *On Participation*. Los Angeles: Law In A Free Society, 1973.

Reedy, George E. *The Twilight of the Presidency*. New York and Cleveland: The World Publishing Company, 1970.

Rosenbloom, David Lee. *The Election Men: Professional Campaign Managers and American Democracy*. New York: Quadrangle, 1973.

*Roseboom, Eugene Holloway and Alfred E. Eckes. *A History of Presidential Elections*. New York: Macmillan Publishing Co., Inc., 1979.

*Russell, Francis. *The President Makers*. Boston/Toronto: Little Brown and Company, 1976.

Saul, Mort. *Heartland*. New York and London: Harcourt Brace Jovanovich, 1976.

*Sandoz, Ellis and Cecil V. Crabb, eds. *A Tide of Discontent: The 1980 Elections and Their Meaning*. Washington, D.C.: Congressional Quarterly Press, 1981.

Seldes, George. *Freedom of the Press*. Indianapolis/New York: The Bobbs-Merrill Company, Publishers, 1935.

*Sherrill, Robert. *Gothic Politics in the Deep South*. New York: Grossman Publishers, 1968.

Sinkler, George. *The Racial Attitudes of American Presidents*. Garden City, New York: Doubleday & Company, Inc., 1971.

*Spero, Robert. *The Duping of the American Voter*. New York: Lippincott & Crowell, Publishers, 1980.

Stearn, Gerald Emanuel, ed. *Broken Image: Foreign Critiques of America*. New York: Random House, 1972.

Bibliography

*Steffens, Lincoln. *The Shame of the Cities*. New York: Hill and Wang, 1957.

*Thompson, Hunter S. *Fear and Loathing on the Campaign Trail '72*. New York: Popular Library, 1974.

*Weingast, David E. *We Elect A President*. New York: Julian Messner, 1966.

*White, Theodore. *America In Search of Itself: The Making of the President 1956–1980*. New York: Harper & Row, Publishers, 1982.

*Wolfinger, Raymond E. and Stephen J. Rosenstone. *Who Votes?* New Haven: Yale University Press, 1980 .

Also consulted were issues of *Newsweek*, *The Nation*, *Reader's Digest*, *Life*, *Commonsense*, *Variety*, the *Australian National Times*, *American Civil Liberties Union* reports, and political materials provided by various political parties.

INDEX

Index

Index

Index

Index